THE "WHAT WORKS" METHOD

THE "WHAT WORKS" METHOD

A Process for Learning

Elizabeth F. Swanson, EdD, Editor
with Mark N. Ozer, MD

Every mind must know the whole lesson for itself, must go over the whole ground. What it does not see, what it does not live, it will not know.

Ralph Waldo Emerson

SPECIAL CHILD PUBLICATIONS / SEATTLE

Special Child Publications
J. B. Preston, Editor & Publisher
P. O. Box 33548
Seattle, Washington 98133

Serving the special child since 1962

International Standard Book Number: 0-87562-089-2

94 93 92 91 90 89 88 87
10 9 8 7 6 5 4 3 2

Contents

We wish to acknowledge all those teachers, parents, and students who shared with us in the development of this book. We have in common the desire to restore the integrity of the educational process, to return education to the realm of individual responsibility and meaningful learning.

Many thanks to Irene Strack and Richard Gold for their editorial expertise and personal insight in helping this book come to fruition.

Thanks also to John Niles, Frances Fuchs, and Nancy Taylor for their assistance in reviewing chapters and making useful suggestions that added to the quality of the final product.

Preface

Mark N. Ozer, MD

This volume marks the independent application by my colleagues in their various educational settings of ideas which I have evolved since 1965 in dealing with issues of assessment and treatment of children with learning problems. What is here called the "What Works" method is a program I have previously written about as the Problem Solving Planning System (PSPS).

As the director of the Program for Learning Studies at the Childrens Hospital National Medical Center in Washington, D.C., I had the opportunity to work with an interdisciplinary group of people who were concerned with going beyond the narrow sense of diagnosis. The first concern was to go beyond the traditional categorization of children with developmental problems toward what I called an "operational diagnosis." Instead of categorizing children in terms of "brain injured" or "emotionally disturbed," I felt that it was necessary to describe the problems which the child had in his learning in terms of the actual difficulties he had in his day-to-day work. Once the problem was stated in terms of the observed difficulty (for example, in reading or math or behavior), the people involved could then develop a direct plan for solving such problems. One product of the assessment would be a set of goals derived from the direct observation of the child in his natural setting.

My second concern with the traditional format for assessment of children was the degree to which those who were most directly involved with the child were excluded from the assessment process. The various specialists traditionally responsible for the diagnostic assessment all have a rather time-limited and narrow sample of the child's behavior in the educational setting. It's clear, meanwhile, that those who are involved in a more ongoing and broader relationship with the child are what I called the "primary participants" in a long-term treatment of the child. If the assessment by the educational specialist is not merely to lead to some sort of categorization but rather a plan for treatment, then the *process* by which the plan was generated would need to change. The specialist would begin to take a role of consultant to the primary participants: the regular classroom teacher, the parents, and the child. I began to see that the very process of planning, if properly designed, could lead to the enhancement of the confidence and competence of these primary persons, and that, ultimately, it was the child who would have to take the primary role in his own learning. It was the child who must ultimately discover the ways by which he may be able to solve for himself the problems he had in his learning.

My third concern was with the discontinuity between the assessment of the child and the actual implementation of the plans that arose out of that assessment. The traditional approach has been to see the planning process as leading to an educational plan, with a subsequent evaluation of the degree of accomplishment and the making of a new plan at a time quite removed from the original process. My view was that the process of planning, evaluation, and recycling could be accomplished on a day to day basis integral to the educational program. The cycle could go on daily, weekly, monthly, or whatever, but the process of review and planning would not be limited to some one time alone. The very activity of planning, if properly conceived, could become an integral unit of the curriculum; with the child eventually carrying out the procedure on his own. In addition to learning how to read or compute, the student would learn how to plan his educational program as he must increasingly do during the course of his educational career.

It is this last aspect which is particularly reflected in this book. Here it is exemplified how the planning process I developed can be used in a variety of educational settings, in day to day work with children, as well as in an assessment generally separate from the instructional program. From the start of my work in conjunction with educators, I was concerned with how one might provide a structure for changing the daily activities carried out between teacher and specialists as well as between teacher and student. It seemed to me that the procedures carried out not merely seek to achieve the development of the child as some far-off goal but support its accomplishment in every interaction. It seemed particularly important to take this more self-conscious approach with those children for whom the educational programs were relatively unsuccessful. It is with those children who have learning and behavioral difficulties in the standard instructional program that it becomes crucial that the child take an increasingly independent role in his own learning. The standard prescriptions do not work, and the various special educational programs have failed to provide a vehicle for the participation of the child in solving his own problems.

The procedures I developed that are illustrated throughout this book are an attempt to provide such a structure in which there can be far greater awareness of the content and form of the interaction leading to independent function of the student. By content, I mean what one talks about with the child; by form, I mean how one goes about talking.

The usual things one talks about with a student have to do with what

I call the "state" of things. The teacher and the student frequently talk about whether something is correct or incorrect; about how much or how little; about the *what*'s. In the planning model I developed to solve learning problems, I did seek data about the "state" of the learning situation. I thought it was useful to talk about what was not going well and what was going well. I also thought it was important to describe what might be some goals for the future. However, I added the discussion of the *how* rather than only the *what*. When one talks about the *how* by which things may occur, an important new dimension is added to the conversation. Although one may have a multitude of tasks that may change somewhat from day to day, the way one goes about doing those tasks is generally far less changeable. I also came to think that the place to seek such information was in the context of those situations, however rare, when there had been at least some degree of success in meeting one's goal—the times when things had gone well. It was in the context of those times that the child may most profitably seek to find ideas that one might wish to use in the future.

The usual order in which one talks is to describe a problem—the things that are not going well—and then move to set goals for the future to alleviate that problem. I felt it necessary to intercalate the experience of what had gone well and how that might have occurred, and to do this *after* the description of the problem and *before* the making of goals for the future. It seemed to me that it would be easier to envisage the possibility of doing something in the future if one recaptured some of those experiences which were even partially successful. Further, the exploration of how those successes may have occurred would provide useful ideas as to how the goals might be accomplished. These two new things to talk about both provided hope and a greater sense of the ways by which that hope might be realized.

As one works with a child in the context of any educational interaction, the child frequently begins to find what may be a clearer indication of what does work for him. In a number of situations from day to day, he may find the same ideas working again and again. For example, a child may find it helpful to verbalize to himself what he hears to be better able to recall it. He may have noted that strategy one time when he was able to recall the instructions the teacher told the class. On still another occasion, he may have found it helpful in remembering what the soccer coach said to him and so on.

The recurrent discussion of what may have worked may elicit not just one idea again and again. The idea of repeating what one hears as it is being said may have worked on several occasions. However, at still another time when recalling a number, the child may have found it helpful to write down what was being said as a way of recalling it. On still another occasion, it may have appeared helpful to move to the front of the room where there were fewer distractions. What becomes more and more evident is that there are ways that work that have general applicability; and that there are such a number of them that, if one way does not work, a person may try another. I have found it useful in this regard to develop an awareness in the child of the possible alternatives by building a repertoire of at least three such strategies. Strategies may vary from time to time, and increasingly the child becomes more aware of the possibility of alternative ways of doing things. It is the sense of options which is being engendered; that if one way doesn't work, there are others. I will defer until later a description of the format by which these ideas are elicited increasingly from the child.

In addition to an awareness of sometimes rather mundane but highly useful strategies, some rather exciting breakthroughs occur when the child feels free to describe and use what may be very individualistic approaches. It is frequently a rather playful idea about what works which provides the solution for the serious problems. I can recall a teenager with major reading and language difficulties, difficulties that had defied the most creative teaching techniques available. He began rather surprisingly to gain several grades in reading when he stated that he could conceptualize the book he was reading to be like a movie. He described in vivid detail the way he was visualizing the ideas he was hearing as he read aloud. Still another boy, a ten-year-old, was able to remain seated in class when he told me he imagined that he had sprayed some Elmer's glue on the seat. He described how he had actually gone through the motions of doing so several times before he was able to just think about doing so. Still another, even younger, boy comes to mind who had particular problems in handwriting. He was able to learn to write in cursive by saying it looked like "an escalator going up and an elevator coming down" in writing his letters. These ideas were valuable in providing solutions for these students who had previously not been able to solve their problems. I have felt that their value for these individuals lay not merely in the elegance of the ideas but in their source—the fact that they had come from the students themselves.

It is the ability of the child to be aware of the ways which work for him, and his self-instruction in their use, that provides the solution. How can the form of the interaction between the adult and the child enhance the likelihood of that internalization of instruction?

One factor contributing to increasing participation on the part of the child was to recognize the degree to which such participation was indeed occurring. If the child were told how to do something by the teacher, the acquiescence of the child to the instruction provided a rather low level of participation. To enhance the likelihood that the child will instruct himself in a similar fashion in the future and carry out the strategy independently, a different format was used that permitted a greater degree of contribution. MacKay (in the book *Information, Mechanism and Meaning* published by MIT Press in 1969) has been particularly useful in helping me to define such a contribution based upon an awareness of the grammatical structure of the interaction. The giving of an instruction has the quality of a "command." It has what MacKay called an "imperative" aspect which claims control over both the thoughts and actions of the recipient. Quite a different message is conveyed by the use of a *question* which invites the recipient to potentially affect the questioner. The questioner is stating, "I do not really know what your answer might be to this. I need your help." Indeed the teacher cannot know without the student's response what might be the latter's state of knowledge about any subject. In the context of the problem solving planning approach described here, the teacher cannot know without the participation of the child what the child feels good about, what he feels bad about, and so on. The child ultimately must learn to speak for himself, and the use of questions rather than instructions permits such independent function to occur.

If the highest level of contribution is for the child to speak entirely for himself, the lowest is when the child is offered an already formulated answer to which he may agree or disagree. The contribution on the part of the child remains rather small when merely a nod of "yes" or "no" need be expressed. On the other hand, the verbalization of what has been agreed upon (confirmed agreement), in my opinion, marks a significant shift in the likelihood that the child may later be able to instruct himself again in the future. Still greater contribution is available if the child is able to select from among several instructional alternatives. The degree of independent function represented by the ability to choose from alternatives and to verbalize one's choice makes still more likely a replication of such statements in other situations. The effect of the interaction can thus be determined at least in part by the use of questions and the degree to which the answers are formulated in advance by the teacher. An awareness of this continuum is helpful to enable the child to function at the highest level consistent with the requirements of the situation. (These issues are dealt with in far greater detail in my book *Solving Learning and Behavior Problems of Children* published by Jossey-Bass in 1980.)

Although the use of questions enables the child to contribute to the interaction, the reception of the child's answers by the other is another important factor in the growth of the ability of the child to develop his own answers. The entire process is a dialogue in which there are no "right" or "wrong" answers to these basic questions. It is necessary eventually for the child to learn to reflect upon himself and to learn how to continue to explore his own ways of learning by himself.

A learning experience of my own has helped me to see the mechanism by which this can occur. I was in a workshop where the participants were learning to become aware of their own feelings. I found this task very difficult. The instructor served as a "consultant" in this setting and would make comments about the character of the interactions that were going on in the small group. I found his comments cryptic and in no way reflective of my own experience for several sessions until he said something that was very clear to me. I heard him reflect on something which I had said. I was able to hear him. I felt that there was evidence that I had been heard and I was concurrently able to hear him.

That is the crucial aspect of a dialogue. There must not only be a sharing of experience and ideas. There must be evidence that such sharing is going on. I believe that giving the child evidence that he is being heard enables the child to hear himself and eventually internalize both the answers and the questions. Such evidence may be made available to the child in a number of ways. One way might be the actual repetition of the statement made prior to reacting to it. For example, the likelihood of the child being aware of and using again the strategy of the "escalator and elevator" metaphor increases when his statement is fed back or otherwise reflected upon. Still another format for providing such evidence is a technique described by some of the authors in this book of recording on paper what is being said in open view of the person speaking. I have found it useful to not only record the answers in this way but give a copy of the questions and answers to the other person to take with him. The existence of a dialogue thus requires not only at least two people attending to one another, but their giving explicit evidence of doing so.

This book, entitled *The "What Works" Method*, serves to illustrate the use of the questioning process and the use of a specific set of questions. It illustrates how those questions can bring about an awareness of some needed answers, and how those answers may arise increasingly from the learner. In the process of searching for answers, the learner becomes more aware that there are indeed answers, that answers can change, and that what is particularly useful is to keep asking these very questions on one's own.

This book arose out of a series of interactions with persons in the field of education over a number of years. Each person had the opportunity to hear about my work and then use the basic principles in his or her own individual setting. In the writing of this book, the authors of the various chapters also add new dimensions to my understanding of how the basic approach may be adapted to situations far beyond my own opportunity to do so. It is for their contributions to my own development that I am grateful. I hope that the potential universality of the method will become evident, that others may in turn adapt the approach to their own settings, and that these modifications may be the basis for many future books.

Mark N. Ozer
Richmond, Virginia

An Introduction to "What Works"

Elizabeth F. Swanson, EdD

A RESPONSE TO THE EDUCATIONAL CHALLENGE OF THE '80s

The "What Works" Method introduces a new and well-tested approach to solving educational problems in assessment and instruction. The systematic steps of the system will help educators to work more effectively with each other and with students. The book illustrates the use of this system with a variety of students experiencing learning and behavior problems in elementary school, junior high, high school, and college. This book addresses the application of this system by regular and special education classroom teachers; by multidisciplinary team members such as special educators, psychologists, and counselors; and by educators who serve in consulting roles such as resource teachers, speech therapists, and reading specialists. The chapter authors describe their years of experience applying "What Works" in classroom instruction, team decision-making, the inservice training of teachers, and college counseling.

The "What Works" Method addresses a major problem facing American teaching at this time, that of delivering quality education while also meeting the instructional needs of an increasingly heterogeneous student body in an increasingly complex society. This is a problem described by the National Commission on Excellence in Education (NCEE 1983). The final report of this commission cites declining achievement scores, high numbers of functionally illiterate adults, and the lack of "higher order" intellectual skills among many secondary students. These findings are indicators of risks that threaten the well-being of this country (NCEE 1983, p.8):

> Part of what is at risk is the promise first made on this continent: All, regardless of race or class or economic status, are entitled to a fair chance and to the tools for developing their individual powers

of mind and spirit to the utmost. This promise means that all children by virtue of their own efforts, competently guided, can hope to attain the mature and informed judgment needed to secure gainful employment and to manage their own lives, thereby serving not only their own interests but also the progress of society itself.

Increasingly, our schools and colleges enroll students with varied backgrounds, learning characteristics, and levels of achievement. More minority groups are enrolled in public schools today than in the past. More students who are handicapped, both physically and intellectually, are enrolled in regular classes. Although entitled to an education on the basis of law and public policy, many of these students consistently have difficulty mastering the curriculum as it is traditionally taught. The educational system has reacted to this increasing heterogeneity by categorizing atypical students and offering separate programs. This trend has encouraged unnecessary segregation of many students from their peers and has become a financial burden to the educational system.

A growing body of research suggests that the multiplicity of categorical programs has led to a number of problems:

- Instructional classifications are not based upon the characteristics of the student but rather upon the values of the educational system. In New York City a few years ago, approximately 30 percent of its students of Puerto Rican background were enrolled in special education classes (Smith 1980). Other school districts have used tracking systems to segregate such minorities as Blacks and Hispanics. The number and proportion of children from minority backgrounds occupying special education classes for any instructional classification often varies dramatically from one school district to another. This form of segregation is often attributed to bias in the assessment process (Duffey, Salvia, Tucker, and Ysseldyke 1981). One approach to this form of segregation is to eliminate disability labels and categories and merge special with regular education into a more unified system which addresses the unique learning needs of all students (Stainback and Stainback 1984; Wang and Reynolds 1985).
- There is no conclusive evidence that segregated programs for most categories of special student are more effective than instructing those students in the regular classroom (Carlberg and Kavale 1980). Furthermore, the gains accomplished by separating students from their assigned regular classes will be minimal or nonexistent unless considerable effort at integration and transfer of learning occurs among programs. To be successful, integration must include the coordination of the special instruction with that content being taught in the regular setting, communication among the professionals working with the same student, and efforts to help students transfer their learning from one setting to another.
- The costs of identifying students for separate coursework and of administrative maintenance of such separate programs are exces-

sive. Admission to special programs usually entails hours of classification procedures on the part of instructional specialists and extensive paperwork on the part of administrators (Reynolds 1982). Furthermore, this process serves only administrative decisions and provides little benefit to the student's instructional program in the classroom (Idol-Maestas, Lloyd, and Lilly 1981).

The growing opinion of teacher educators is that the body of knowledge, skills, and attitudes required for success in teaching "special" groups of students is the same for the teachers of students in the regular classroom (Zigmond and Sansone 1981). Regular teachers can learn to individualize and to adapt their programs to a variety of learners in the classroom if they do not do so already (McCormick 1979). There are clearly more differences within any given group of students than there are differences between those in any two groups.

Research suggests that good teaching draws from students their own resources and self-sufficiency in the educational process (Ozer 1980). Good teaching is also characterized by cooperative goal setting between the teacher and students (Johnson and Johnson 1975). This means setting appropriate instructional goals, differentiating curriculum materials, grouping students appropriately, and knowing a variety of approaches for reaching any given instructional goal (McDonald 1977). All these qualities not only assist the so-called ordinary student but also accommodate those students whom educators have tended to label as "different" in recent years. With the exception of those students most severely handicapped, good teaching practice as found in many regular settings would be appropriate for a far greater range of students with their varied learning characteristics.

THE "WHAT WORKS" METHOD

The "What Works" method involves five basic dialogue questions:

1. *What is the student's problem?* Too often teachers are overwhelmed by the many failures of a problem learner, or a team cannot come to agreement on the most immediate needs of the student needing assistance. This question and its related sub-steps allows the problem solver (student, teacher, or team) to identify a specific, manageable concern that, once resolved, would begin to lead the problem learner toward a more successful school experience.
2. *What has gone well for you in the area of concern?* This question encourages the problem solver to reflect back upon earlier experiences to discover instances of past success in the area of concern. At first teachers tend to see nothing positive about students who have caused them persistent problems in the classroom. This question turns around that point of view by directing teachers to focus on any positive attribute of the student in relation to the problem area, whether it be the few words in reading that the student does know or the few times when he has behaved ap-

propriately in class. In relation to student use of the method, it directs the user to focus not upon persistent failures of the past, but upon instances where there has been success. This focus helps to change the self-concept of failure which so typically pervades the thinking of students who do not experience success in school.

The problem solver is encouraged to generate at least three responses to this question. In the case of a student who has difficulty thinking of successful experiences, the teacher may request to contribute to the responses to this question.

3. *What contributed to these successes? What worked?* Here the problem solver analyzes past successful experiences to determine how they came about. This question leads to an awareness of strategies that can be used to address the current area of concern.

   This is a key question which differentiates the "What Works" method from other problem solving approaches. The question draws upon the problem solver's self-knowledge about what works for him. Through the process of *brainstorming*, then *selection* of previously successful strategies, individuals become aware of how their thinking enables them to be successful in related experiences. This question stimulates an active process of self-exploration and provides problem solvers with the tools they need to solve new and more difficult problems. Increasingly these tools come from within the individual as he achieves more responsibility for his own learning.
4. *What do you want to see happen?* Having selected a concern and analyzed it in light of past successful experiences in the area, the problem solver now thinks about what he wants to see happen in the future. This is a goal-setting question in which the student, teacher, or team begins to visualize the end result, the problem in its resolved form.
5. *How can you make it happen? Make a plan.* The problem solver draws upon what he has learned about the issue of concern in the previous questions. He develops a plan which applies previously successful strategies to current concerns.

The "What Works" method is a cyclical process in which evaluation is a critical component. Evaluation enables the problem solver to modify his plan in the face of changing conditions and events. Evaluation allows for ongoing refinement of a plan. It also provides information that can be used in the formulation of new plans.

The problem solver always evaluates the results of the "What Works" plan in light of the goals set in question 4. If the goals are not achieved, a new plan is developed based upon current review. If the plan is successful, then the problem solver repeats the process, using the "What Works" questions to address another concern about the problem learner.

Mark N. Ozer, who developed the "What Works" method (which he has earlier called the Problem Solving Planning System), describes this method as a way of increasing responsibility for self-directed action in the problem solver. In the case of the teacher working with a student, "What Works" provides them with a vehicle, a dialogue, both for solving a specific problem and for allowing the student the freedom to make choices and increase his awareness of what behaviors or what learning strategies work for him. Ozer states (1983, p.19):

> The teacher is functioning in the role of helping the child to grow in his awareness of himself and his ability to take responsibility for his own learning . . . Each educational interaction has potentially the opportunity not only to achieve some specific task. In the context of the child learning any task, the child may have the opportunity to learn about himself . . .

Using the "What Works" method is not something that occurs spontaneously between teacher and student, just as introduction of the open classroom concept did not spontaneously develop self-directed learning in students. The teacher must carefully structure the dialogue with students so that they gradually begin to internalize the questions for their later use. More structure will be required with students who do not readily use systematic methods for learning new material in school. The teacher acts as a model for these students, demonstrating a method whereby independent learning can occur. To again quote Ozer (1983, p.35):

> The instructor, by serving as a resource in the dialogue . . . has provided a model for the student for the entire process—the questions to be asked, their order, the steps of exploration and selection as well as providing specific ideas in answer to any of the questions. In this fashion, there may be internalization not only of the answers to the planning questions but the ability eventually (for the student) to ask the questions for oneself . . .

Many teachers are uncomfortable using a dialogue such as this, which necessarily requires that they give up a degree of control in order that the student may experience some freedom in choosing a plan of action for his own learning. But if growth in personal responsibility is considered an important goal in education, then teachers must be willing to risk to the extent that they allow students the opportunity to grow by sharing in the responsibility of education.

PLAN OF THE BOOK

The "What Works" Method shows educators how to answer the five problem solving questions themselves and how to help students answer them. Using this format, a decision-making team can solve the perplexing problems of student assessment and instructional planning. "What Works" can serve as a basis of communication between teacher consultants, such as resource teachers and other educational specialists, and the regular teacher who plays the primary role in the student's instructional program.

The chapter entitled *"What Works" for Students*, by Elizabeth Barger, addresses the needs of teachers who work with increasingly heterogeneous groups of students and who can no longer rely upon a standard curriculum to be taught in the same way to all students. This chapter tells how the "What Works" method can be used as a tool to promote greater responsibility of students for their own instructional programs, thus lessening the demands made upon the teacher for the individualized instruction of each student.

The chapter entitled *"What Works" with Interdisciplinary Teams*, by Harriet Liebow, shows how the method can help a team come to agreement about the issues of primary concern in relation to a problem student. This chapter illustrates a systematic approach for dealing with those identified concerns and for drawing relevant data from all team members, including parents and student, in mutually understandable language.

The chapter entitled *Transferring "What Works" to the Regular Classroom*, by Ruth E. Harris, addresses the needs of educational specialists who teach students in a setting apart from the regular classroom or who act as consultants to regular teachers. This chapter describes ways the educational specialist can use the "What Works" method to enable such students to work more effectively in the regular classroom setting.

The chapter entitled *Inservice: "What Works" with Learning Problems*, by Elizabeth F. Swanson and Nancy Smith, concerns the application of "What Works" to the inservice training of regular teachers who work with students experiencing learning and behavior difficulties in their classrooms. This chapter shows how the problem solving dialogue can be applied to both the content and process of inservice training programs.

The chapter entitled *"What Works" in College Counseling*, by Ruth Talbott Keimig, describes how to use "What Works" in a counseling program with students experiencing academic difficulties. The role of the counselor using this method is to assist students with problems through a self-discovery of strategies that have worked in other learning situations. These strategies are then incorporated into an instructional plan dealing with the problem area. The application described by Dr. Keimig serves as a counseling model for both secondary and college level instructional settings.

Finally, the chapter entitled *Thinking About "What Works,"* by Elizabeth F. Swanson, calls for a return to the original meaning of the word "education," which is "to lead forth." This chapter reviews current research in problem solving and its relationship to academic achievement. This chapter stresses the importance of helping both students and educators draw upon their own inner resources to solve the instructional problems facing them. The result is mutual responsibility on the part of teachers and students for the achievement of educational goals.

REFERENCES

Carlberg, C., and Kavale, K. 1980. The efficacy of special versus regular class placement for exceptional children: a meta-analysis. *The Journal of Special Education* 14:3, pp. 295-309.

Duffey, J. B., Salvia, J., Tucker, J., and Ysseldyke, J. 1981. Nonbiased assessment: a need for operationalism. *Exceptional Children* 47:6, pp. 427-434.

Idol-Maestas, L., Lloyd, S., and Lilly, M. S. 1981. A noncategorical approach to direct service and teacher education. *Exceptional Children* 48:3, pp. 213-220.

Johnson, D. W., and Johnson, R. T. 1975. *Learning together and alone*. Englewood Cliffs, New Jersey: Prentice-Hall.

McDonald, F. J. 1977. Research and development strategies for improving teacher education. *Journal of Teacher Education* 28:6, pp. 29-33.

McCormick, W. J. 1979. Teachers can learn to teach more effectively. *Educational Leadership* 37:1, pp. 59-60.

National Commission on Excellence in Education. 1983. An open letter to the American people. A nation at risk: the imperative for educational reform. Washington, D. C.: U. S. Government Printing Office.

Ozer, M. N. 1983. *The dialogue of education.* Unpublished manuscript.

Ozer, M. N. 1980. *Solving learning and behavior problems of children*. San Francisco: Jossey-Bass.

Reynolds, M. 1982. *A look to the future*. Paper presented at annual meeting of Deans' Grant Projects. Minneapolis.

Smith, A. M. 1980. Reaction: toward an enlargement of general principles. In *A common body of practice for teachers: the challenge of Public Law 94-142 to teacher education*, produced by The National Support Systems Project, pp. 79-89. Washington, D. C.: The American Association of Colleges of Teacher Education.

Stainback, W., and Stainback, S. 1984. A rationale for the merger of special and regular education. *Exceptional Children* 51:2, pp. 102-111.

Wang, M. C., and Reynolds, M. 1985. Avoiding the "catch 22" in special education reform. *Exceptional Children* 51:6, pp. 497-502.

Zigmond, N., and Sansone, J. 1981. What we know about mainstreaming from experience. In *Mainstreaming: our current knowledge base*, ed. P. Bates, pp. 97-111. Minneapolis: National Support Systems Project, University of Minnesota.

"What Works" for Students

Elizabeth Barger, EdD

The critical ability to manage curriculum content and such constraints as time, materials, and facilities, along with the needs of the various students in the class is what differentiates effective from ineffective teachers. At one time it was considered acceptable for a teacher to use the same method and activities for all students in the class. However, with more mildly handicapped students in regular classrooms and an otherwise increasing heterogeneity in class make-up (Lord 1974; Lewis and Doorlag 1983), this single-plan method of instruction is fast becoming inappropriate for most classrooms. Teachers now face greater differences in the instructional needs of their students. To cope with these differences, conscientious teachers often believe that they must diagnose every student's needs in all academic areas and develop multiple individualized methods for reaching each instructional goal. This approach is cumbersome and requires an excessive amount of planning time. It also falsely assumes that one can accurately match diagnostic test results with appropriate instructional strategies (Ozer 1980).

One way to meet the variety of student needs in a heterogeneous classroom grouping is to encourage students to share the responsibility of instructional planning. This shifts much of the burden from teacher to students, who then play active roles in the development of (1) their instructional plans, (2) the strategies for implementing these plans, and (3) the criteria for evaluating their outcomes. When teachers share this responsibility with students, these tasks often lead to greater academic achievement, improved communication skills, and more accepting attitudes on the part of students toward individual differences.

The growth in academic achievement resulting from classroom interactions (teacher-pupil and pupil-pupil) has been documented by several researchers. In his research on "Teacher Influence, Pupil Attitude, and Achievement," Flanders (1971) concluded that higher standards can be achieved by asking students questions and by using student ideas, perceptions, and reactions to build greater student self-direction. Teaching then becomes a process of communication between teacher and student, with greater learning efficiency the result. David Aspy studied the relationship between pupils' reading achievement and the presence of teachers' "interchangeable statements," defined as a response which shows that the teacher has heard and understood the student completely and accurately. Pupils of teachers high in the number of interchangeable responses scored better than pupils of teachers low in the number of interchangeable responses. Several follow-up studies by Aspy continued to support this theme, suggesting that teachers who pay careful attention to their students and who listen to what they have to say produce greater achievement than teachers who interact with a low number of interchangeable statements (Good, Biddle, and Brophy 1976).

With recent trends toward the use of self-paced materials and independent activities, the importance of group interaction in the classroom has been understressed (Hennings 1978). Structured communication not only plays an important role in student language development but can be used to set the stage for curriculum adaptations to meet individual needs. The teacher who offers students opportunities to express their needs, their learning preferences, and their desire to help each other learn, thereby acquires practical information for instructional planning and enhances students' communication skills and achievement.

Group participation in the learning process increases academic achievement and encourages acceptance of individual differences (Slavin 1981). While steps have been taken in recent years to bring together students of different races or ethnic backgrounds, these students do not automatically form friendships or interact amicably with each other. Neither do mainstreamed students with learning problems necessarily bridge the social and academic gaps between themselves and their academically achieving peers. However, studies that use a variety of cooperative learning models in which students assist each other on an equal footing to reach specified academic goals, have shown positive effects on improving relationships between students of different ethnic backgrounds. These effects tended to persist over time. Students who experienced cooperative learning had significantly more friends from different ethnic backgrounds than did students who learned by traditional methods of instruction (Slavin 1981). Likewise, an increase in interaction on the part of mainstreamed students with their normally achieving peers led to an increase in friendships between the two groups (Slavin, Madden, and Leavey 1982). Furthermore, the rejection of academically handicapped students by normal achievers in the regular classroom decreased (Madden and Slavin 1982).

Much has been written about flexible grouping, individualized instruction, independent study, and the open setting. What must now be emphasized is individualized learning. A student is motivated to learn when the content material is meaningful and is presented at a level which meets the student's developmental needs. Dialogue between teacher and students can provide the instructional method needed to accommodate the curriculum to a student's needs.

USING THE "WHAT WORKS" METHOD IN THE CLASSROOM

The "What Works" method is a vehicle for formalizing or programming instruction which allows the teacher and students to share in the responsibility of instruction. The system draws upon individual concerns and resources to achieve instructional goals. Likewise, it provides the guidance and structure needed by the student to assist in the learning process. What differentiates this method from other approaches to problem solving is its use of the students' previously successful experiences to determine strategies for mastering current learning material. This is accomplished through the flexible use of the five key problem solving questions:

1. *What are some things you do (very) well?* or *What are some things you do well in (subject)?*

   What else do you do well?
   Tell me another thing you do well.
   Which of these things do you feel best about?
   Which of these things are you most proud of?

2. *What helped you to learn to do these things well?*

   What helped you the most?
   Name *all* the things that helped you (again).

3. *What are some things that are hard for you to do?*

   What else is hard for you?
   Tell me a little bit more about your problem?
   What gives you the *most* trouble?

4. *What things do you want to see happen?*

   What are your goals?
   What do you want to work on first?
   What do you think we should do tomorrow?

5. *How can you achieve your goal?*

   What is your plan?

These five questions form the basic structure for a dialogue between students and teacher. They are a guide for interaction, a method which helps teachers and students to clarify their instructional needs, to review material they have mastered, and to determine the learning strategies which caused past achievement. These previously successful strategies can then be applied to efficient learning in a new plan which builds upon the material students already know. In this process, students learn to draw upon their self-knowledge for information about what they know, how they learn, what is needed in the future, and how they will accomplish their goals. This is a problem solving instructional planning system which becomes internalized by students through its use. As the guiding questions become familiar through repeated use, students begin to apply this method to other problem areas, thus increasing their opportunities for academic success.

The "What Works" dialogue can be used in three areas of classroom management: to help students formulate their own learning strategies; to introduce a lesson or unit; and to help students summarize and evaluate their work. Described below are examples of each of the three uses of the "What Works" method in the classroom.

Formulating Learning Strategies

The teacher can use the "What Works" dialogue to help students become aware of their successful learning strategies. With this knowledge, students then develop plans to use these strategies in new learning activities. In the following example, the teacher worked with a small group of students whose quality of written work was poor and who had difficulty completing written assignments. The teacher wanted the students to improve their writing skills and do their written work more independently in the classroom. This particular "What Works" interaction was used as a diagnostic tool to assess student strengths and needs in the area of written expression. Although students had often been asked to do creative writing and had received some supervised instruction related to writing sentences, simple paragraphs, and letters, the students had many weaknesses in this area. "What Works" was used to answer the question: "What do the students perceive their weaknesses to be relative to writing paragraphs or stories?" A simple variation of the first dialogue question was used to initiate the problem solving process with this group of fifth grade pupils:

Teacher:	*What have you learned about writing a paragraph?*
Dwayne:	Indent.
Richard:	Put commas in right places.
David:	Put capital letters where they're supposed to be.
Richard:	Oh, I know one. Put question marks when you ask something.
Dwayne:	The whole paragraph has to be about one thing.
Teacher:	You've learned a lot of things about paragraph writing. *What helped you learn these things?*
Richard:	The teacher just tells us what to do.
David:	We always have to copy stuff over. The teacher puts red marks on the paper and tells us to fix the paper.
Teacher:	Are you saying it helps for you to rewrite a story and make corrections?
David:	Yeah, sometimes. Sometimes I just get mad at the teacher. *(laughter)*
Teacher:	What else helped you learn the things you know about writing paragraphs? *(shrugs)*
Teacher:	Who can restate the two things we have said helped us learn about writing paragraphs in one sentence?
Dwayne:	It helped us when the teacher told us what to do and when we had to copy our stories to fix them.
Teacher:	You said that nicely, Dwayne. *What things are hard for you to do when writing a paragraph?*

Jeff:	I don't have nothin' to write about.
Richard:	Yeah. I can't think of anything to say and I can't spell the hard words. Then I have to copy the story over.
	(chorus of yeahs)
Teacher:	*What do you want to see happen when you begin writing this new paragraph?*
Dwayne:	For all our writing to be neat.
David:	To have good ideas.
	(silence)
Teacher:	*How may I help you write a good paragraph today?*
Dwayne:	Tell us how to spell words.
David:	Give us hints about what to write.
Teacher:	Do you mean you want me to help you plan the paragraph?
David:	Yes. And to help us remember our things.
Teacher:	What do you mean?
Dwayne:	You know—what to do. Like when you wrote a kind of letter with us all so we would know what to do when we wrote a letter. Remember? We all helped you write it and you wrote it on the board.
Teacher:	*(summarizes strategy)* OK. You've said you want me to help you in two ways: help you plan and help you remember what to do so you write a good paragraph.

After summarizing the writing strategies offered by the students, the teacher introduced the topic of "Halloween costumes" for a brief creative writing assignment. The students brainstormed ideas on the topic, and the teacher's plan included the following elements as a guide:

My Halloween Costume

Costume:

Masks:

Parade:

Funny:

(Each student added his/her own details on these topics.)

The dialogue continued after the plan was completed. The teacher's new goal was to encourage students to verbalize some rules for writing paragraphs:

Teacher:	*What should our plan be for writing the paragraph now that we have listed ideas for the paragraph?*
Dwayne:	Change the ideas into sentences.
David:	Remember to indent the first sentence.
Richard:	Make each paragraph be about one thing.
David:	Use capital letters and periods.

These rules were offered spontaneously by the group. They became the strategies used by the students in their written work. The teacher listed these strategies on the board for the students to refer to as they completed the assignment.

Students in the above dialogue focused on the specific factors contributing to their difficulties with creative writing. They became more aware of what they were able to do successfully and where they needed help. As a group, they decided upon the strategy that would best help them put their thoughts into writing. Finally, the students were able to state a number of rules for writing good paragraphs. The teacher continued to use the "What Works" dialogue with her students. As a result of the teacher defining what helped them learn, the students improved considerably in their writing and completed more assignments in class with greater independence.

It is suggested that new teaching objectives result from the growth of diagnostic information contained in teacher-student dialogues. The students above clearly stated what they thought were the most difficult aspects of writing a paragraph: generating ideas and spelling. Capitalizing on this information, the teacher focused future dialogues on these two topics. Other instructional information found in this dialogue suggests that future lessons emphasize (1) differentiating topic and details and (2) giving direct practice in converting an assignment's focus to a topic sentence while placing details in supporting sentences.

A follow-up dialogue several months later provided a comprehensive review of what the students knew about writing a paragraph. Interestingly, the third "What Works" question, "What do you still find to be hard about writing a paragraph?" resulted in more individual responses, suggesting an increase in the students' knowledge about their own learning strategies.

Richard: I still need practice indenting.
Dwayne: I need to practice putting periods in the sentences. Punctuating?
Melvin: Writing. One thing–I forget to put periods and indent.
Dwayne: I don't know how to spell some of the words.
Chorus: Me too.
David: I think I have good ideas, but I can't write them out.

The students then planned two possible paragraphs as a group, selected the topic which most interested them individually, then wrote the paragraph as an independent assignment. All paragraphs but one included a topic sentence. Paragraphs tended to be longer than those written prior to this dialogue. Sentences were more interesting. All students remembered to indent their paragraphs, and fewer periods and capitals were omitted. Even more significant, all the students completed the assignment without complaining. They all appeared to know what to do and did not raise their hands as frequently to ask for teacher assistance.

In another example, the following "What Works" dialogue occurred when a group of third graders prepared to take a unit test in reading. Allen, always a bit anxious in a test-taking situation, said, "Tests are hard. I wish we didn't have to take them." This comment resulted in an unplanned dialogue which led the students to a number of strategies to help learn unfamiliar words.

Teacher: You've learned a lot about reading, Allen. I don't think this test will be so hard for you. Let's all stop and talk about some of the things we've learned in reading this year. *(Tim's hand is up.)* Tim, *what have you learned to do well in reading?*

Tim: I can read books for fun now.

(The children take turns talking as the teacher writes.)

Trey: I can work out lots of new words by myself.

Judy: I learned to read faster.

Allen: I did too.

Cathy: I get all my work right now. I didn't use to.

George: I can read lots of books now.

Teacher: Good. *What do you think helped you do these things?* Each of you think about what you said you could do well. What helped you do these things?

Cathy: You read our papers with us before we worked on them. Then I could do them.

Teacher: Good. It helped for me to read the papers with you. *(The teacher writes this on the board.)* Trey?

Trey: I can sound out words. I remember my sounds.

Teacher: What helped you remember your sounds?

Trey: I learned them with those games.

Teacher: The games helped you practice your sounds then?

Trey: Yes.

(Teacher writes on board.)

Judy: It helped for you to read with me. It was fun reading a story that way.

Allen: Yeah. Mrs. P. helped us by reading with us, too.

Teacher: So it helped when Mrs. P. or I read with you? *(Writes on board.)*

George: I liked reading for prizes. My mom hears me read every night.

Teacher: How does reading every night help you?

George: I learn my words better when I practice reading.

Teacher: Then, practicing helps you?

George: Yeah. I guess it's kind of like Trey, huh? Only I practiced my words.

Teacher: That seems to be true. Now, let's read together the list of things that seem to help us. *(They read together.) Now, let's talk about why taking a reading test might be hard for some of you.* Allen?

Allen: Sometimes there are new words on the test.

(There is a chorus of "yeah.")

Teacher: Then do you all want to talk about what to do when you see a new word in a sentence?

All: Yes.

Teacher: *(Writes on chart: What to do if you meet a new word)* Who has an idea?

Judy: You could sound it out.

Teacher: Yes. But I think you can do something *before* you try to sound it out. Can you remember something I always have you do first?

Trey: You can say "blank" and read the rest of the words in the sentence. The other words help me think of the word I don't know.

(Teacher writes Trey's comment on the chart so that the chart looks like this:)

What to Do When You Meet a New Word

1. Say "blank" and read the rest of the words in the sentence.

Teacher: Now, Judy, tell us your idea again.

Judy: You can sound the word out.

Teacher: Good. *(Writes on chart.)*

Allen: The pictures might help you think of the word. Then you can read the sentence again to get the word.

Teacher: That's really two ideas, Allen. What's your first idea?

Allen: Look at the pictures to help you think of the word.

Teacher: Good. What was your second idea?

Allen: I forgot. *(Children laugh.)* Oh, yeah. Um, you can read the sentence and get the word.

Teacher: Did you say to read the sentence *again* or just read the sentence?

Allen: Read the sentence again.

Teacher: Very good. We *do* sometimes need to read sentences more than once if we are thinking about them. Any more ideas?

George: Well, you might use a dictionary. But, I don't think we can use a dictionary when we take a test.

Teacher: I think using a dictionary to help you think about a word is a good idea, George. When you take a reading test that goes with your book it's all right to use a dictionary. Does anyone else have an idea?

(The children are quiet.)

Teacher: Then, let's read our chart together so we'll remember what to do if we meet a new word on the test.

(The children read the chart with the teacher.)

What to Do When You Meet a New Word

1. Say "blank" and read the rest of the words in the sentence.
2. Sound the word out.
3. Look at the pictures to help you think of the word.
4. You can read the sentence again and get the word.
5. You can use a dictionary.

In this dialogue, the teacher took advantage of a "teachable moment" as she attended to the worry of one student. She drew all students into the resolution of Allen's fear about taking the reading test by using the "What

Works" dialogue to review some rules for recognizing unfamiliar words. The resulting list of ideas provided a good review, and once more brought to conscious awareness those cognitive strategies which helped the students to become independent readers.

Introducing a Lesson Plan or Unit of Study

Using the five "What Works" questions to introduce a lesson or unit of study capitalizes on students' present knowledge and sets the stage for subsequent lessons while determining what information from the unit must be taught. For example, the "What Works" dialogue was used with a group of sixth graders who were assigned to do research and individualized study about past and present life in the United States. The planning session for the unit began as the teacher turned the title of the unit, "Shaping the Social System," into a variation of the first "What Works" question: "What is meant by a social system?" and "What are some factors which would influence the shaping of a social system?" In short, the teacher was asking "What do you know about this subject?" which is a rewording of the first question in the "What Works" dialogue, "What are some things you do well?" The focus is on the students' acquired knowledge rather than past action. Students were encouraged to give any related response that came to mind. This brainstorming technique allowed for maximum student participation without judgments regarding the quality of each idea. The ideas were written in condensed form on the board using diagrams which suggested spokes of a wheel. Figure 1.1. shows the students' responses to the question "What are some factors which shaped (or threatened) our social system?" A list of ideas would have been appropriate also, as long as students could see their contributions in visual form. These became the basis for further discussion and, finally, the selection of topics for group projects.

A variation of question 2 of the "What Works" dialogue was then introduced to the group: "What helped you learn about these ideas?" The students had been using the dictionaries and surveying available books as they pondered the questions. They listed these strategies spontaneously and added that they could learn more by reading, interviewing people, and looking at film strips. Question 3 was reworded in the following manner: "What kinds of things do we need to learn about life in the United States?" Question 4 became "What do you want to see happen tomorrow?" The answer from the group was "Choose our research topics." The response to question 5 of the "What Works" method, a plan of action, came in a subsequent group meeting. At that time the group developed a list of students and their choices of topics as well as a list of sources where they could locate information to prepare for a presentation.

In the example above, the teacher helped the students prepare to research a topic and assisted them in defining and selecting strategies to complete their research. They gained an understanding of the structure of the subject drawn from the collective knowledge of those in the group. They generated a variety of strategies which could be used to address the selected topics as they developed a research plan. With this kind of indepth planning,

FIGURE 1.1. ***An Example of Student Brainstorming Using "What Works."***

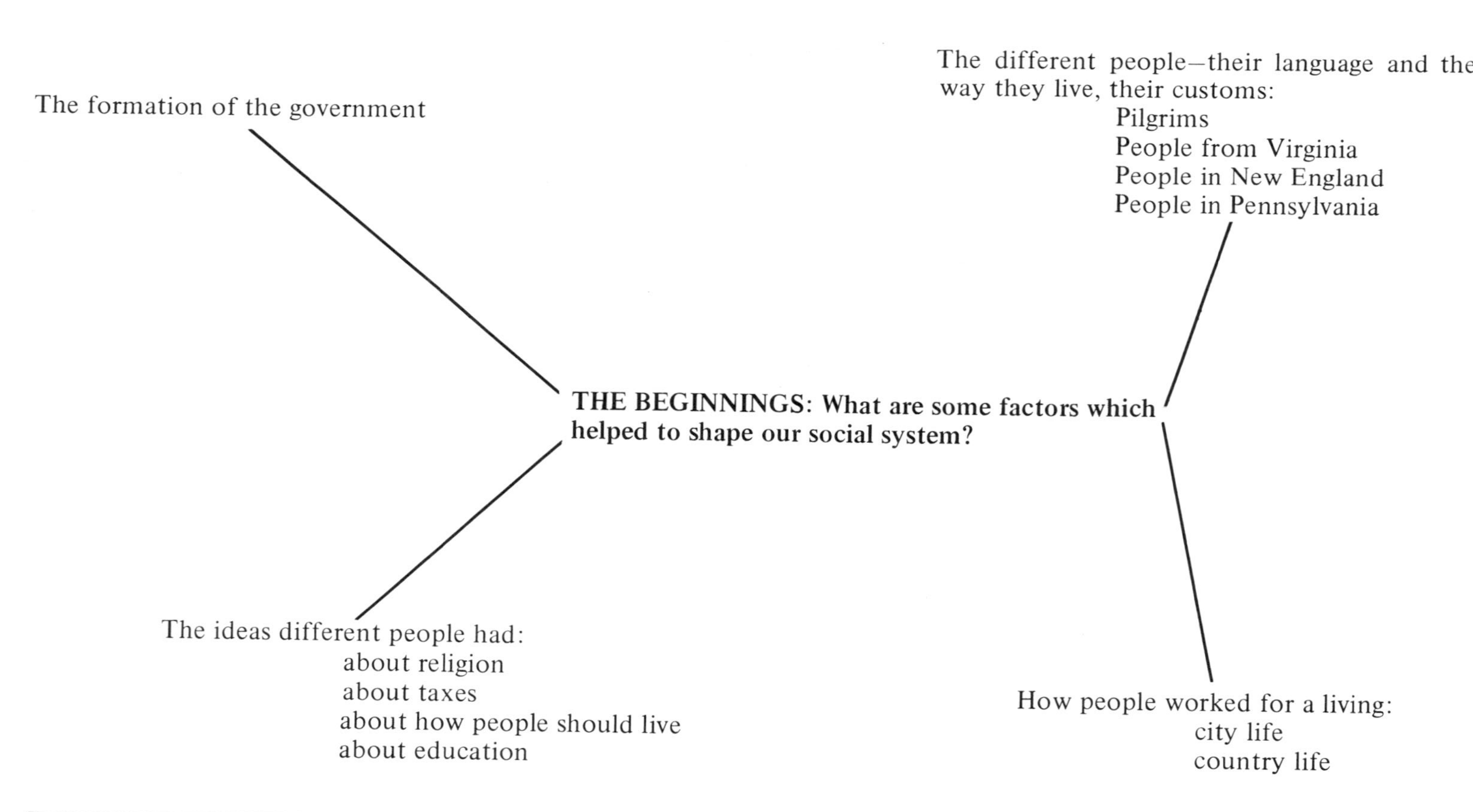

the students successfully completed their research projects with a minimum of teacher assistance; furthermore, their teacher reported that students demonstrated greater independence on other research tasks in the classroom.

A second dialogue example shows how "What Works" can be used to acquire diagnostic information about students' instructional needs when a unit of study is introduced. This dialogue emphasizes the third "What Works" question: What is the problem? A group of fifth graders were introduced to the SQ3R *(Survey, Question, Read, Recite, Review)*, a technique for improving reading comprehension. Using the "What Works" questions, it became apparent that the students lacked a basic conceptual framework for study skills in general. At the beginning of the dialogue, the teacher attempted to draw from them a list of study skills that they knew. Student responses were not spontaneous at first; they could only agree or disagree with an idea presented by the teacher. Gradually, these students began to develop a framework that helped them understand the concepts, although they needed assistance to generate a variety of skills:

Teacher:	What are some study skills you have learned or know about?
Dwayne:	Reading? *(Silence.)* Writing?
Teacher:	Are you *asking* me if reading and writing are study skills?
Dwayne:	I guess so. *(Laughter.)*
Teacher:	Reading and writing are two very important ways we can study or gain information. But other study skills help us to get information which helps us to communicate better when we write. What are some of these study skills? *(Melvin spies the new set of workbooks on the counter—Star Wars: Study Skills.)*
Melvin:	Are those books about study skills?
Teacher:	Yes.
Melvin:	If we could look at those, we might find out what study skills are. *(The workbooks are distributed. There is silence as the boys leaf through the books.)*
Dwayne:	Here's a list of study skills. *(He's looking at the table of contents.)*
Teacher:	OK. Dwayne, give us the page number so we can all look at the list. *(Dwayne complies.)* What is the name of this page?
Dwayne:	Table of Contents.
Teacher:	What information can you get from this page?
Dwayne:	It tells you what is in the book and what page number it's on.
Teacher:	That's right, Dwayne. Now, can anyone name some study skills?
Melvin:	Oh, yeah. Following the directions. *(Hands wave at this point. The boys read the list.)*
Richard:	Locating information.

Jeff:	Dictionary skills.
Dwayne:	Choosing definitions.
Richard:	Learning *about* the table of contents is a study skill, too.
Jeff:	Using a card catalog.
Richard:	Looking at maps.
Dwayne:	Studying graphs.
Melvin:	Making notes and making outlines.
Teacher:	*What kinds of study skills do you think you do well?*
	(Several others are read.)
Dwayne:	Studying graphs.
Melvin:	Following directions.
	(Laughter.)
Jeff:	Using the card catalog.
Richard:	Looking at maps.
Teacher:	*What helped you learn to do these study skills well?*
Dwayne:	Teachers help. Looking up graphs and reading them for Boy Scouts.
Melvin:	The teacher reads the directions and explains what to do.
Jeff:	The teacher helped us learn.
Richard:	Yeah.
Teacher:	*Which study skills are hard for you to do?*
Dwayne:	Writing stories and paragraphs.
Melvin:	Looking at maps.
Richard:	I don't know what definitions mean?
Jeff:	Following directions.
David:	I think taking notes would be hard for me because I don't know what to do.

When asked "What do you want to see happen during our study skills unit?" each student said he wanted to learn the skill he had said would be hard for him. Asked the question "How do you want me to help you learn these skills?" they voted on the sequence of lessons and proposed a plan for each series of lessons. The resulting chart read as follows:

Reading maps

Practice reading maps
Read about maps in the *Star Wars* books

Writing stories

Copy someone's writing
Practice writing words
Use the clock papers to learn how to make our letters better

Making notes

The teacher can read. The children can listen. The teacher can help the children write words to remember the story.

Both teacher and students gained information from this dialogue. The students began to acquire a framework within which they could focus upon developing specific skills. This ability to generalize from part to whole, and to see relationships among parts, would later offer them increasing flexibility in applying a variety of study techniques to different learning tasks. The teacher gained information, too. She realized that her students possessed a limited understanding about what study skills are and how to apply them. This data assisted her in writing subsequent lesson plans for that unit of study. With her knowledge of what the students needed, she then developed specific activities which corresponded to her students' more general ideas.

These students eagerly worked toward completion of their lesson plan. One student located maps outside of school to bring to class for one part of the study unit. This active participation in his own learning was a surprising contrast to his typical reaction, "Do we have to do that?"

Summarizing and Evaluating Student Progress

The five "What Works" questions can be followed with little alteration when this method is used to assist students to summarize or evaluate a day's work or a lesson. In these cases the students' responses give important information about what they believe they learned. Such information helps students and teachers with direction for the next day's lesson. If used regularly, the "What Works" dialogue becomes a diagnostic and prescriptive tool that makes available to students and teacher what has been learned, what is needed, and how individual needs can be met effectively. The dialogue becomes the structure for an ongoing classroom management plan to assist the teacher as students and accomplishments change.

Following is an example of a fifth-grade student with poor spelling performance. Bobby was familiar with the "What Works" process. The teacher had led him through it some weeks earlier in an attempt to help him formulate a strategy for studying unfamiliar words.

Teacher: You got 100 percent on your spelling test today. *What made this happen?*

Bobby: They were compound words. They're pretty easy. I listened to the tape when I watched TV.

Teacher: What did we talk about several weeks ago regarding ways to study spelling?

Bobby: I did it. I gave myself a test. I let the tape say the words and then I spelled them.

Teacher: Did you spell them to yourself or did you write the words?

Bobby: Sometimes I just thought them. Sometimes I wrote them.

Teacher: Which of these helped you the most?

Bobby: Both things helped.

Teacher: What do you mean by both things?

Bobby: Using the tape—listening to the words—and taking the test. I heard a psychiatrist on TV say once that if you play a recorder while you sleep, you'll remember the things on the tape. Do you think that might work for me?

Teacher: It's worth a try. *What are you still having trouble with? Do you think you might have trouble with lesson 33?*

Bobby:	*(After looking at lesson.)* I don't think I'll have trouble. They look pretty easy.
Teacher:	What would you like to see happen now?
Bobby:	Get another 100 percent.
Teacher:	How can we make this happen?
Bobby:	I'm going to push Play and Record, wait 10 minutes so I'll be asleep, then record the words. Then I play the tape recorder while I'm asleep.
Teacher:	What else will you do?
Bobby:	Study them. Just look off the book before the test. I'll play the tape while I watch TV, too. Sometimes I'll play the word, stop it, and spell it.

It was important for Bobby to try out his ideas to determine what study strategies helped him learn to spell. After experimenting with different uses of the tape recorder, he reported that he did best when he listened first to the word spelled on tape, stopped the recorder, and then spelled the word aloud.

As a result of this experience, Bobby began to use the "What Works" method with more proficiency. With teacher guidance he generated an independent plan of action to progress in his spelling.

It is not surprising that the parents of many students whose teachers regularly used the "What Works" dialogue reported that their children were beginning to give them detailed accounts of what they had accomplished. Previously, parents received from their children only a shrug or an "I don't know" or "the same old thing" to any query about what they did in school. The parents stated, in effect, that they felt better informed about the school program and their children seemed more involved in their work.

SUMMARY

"What Works" is a method of classroom management that allows teachers to assess the needs of individuals or groups of students in such a way that the assessment becomes part of an ongoing system of planning and evaluation. The process helps the teacher respond to individual differences—to determine appropriate instructional goals, to adapt curriculum materials, and to vary teaching techniques to meet the diversity of needs in the classroom. This instructional management is accomplished by emphasizing the development of individualized plans in class so that students help to identify their own academic needs and take more responsibility for their own learning. As a result, both teachers and students play more dynamic roles in the instructional process.

REFERENCES

Flanders, N. 1971. Teacher influence, pupil attitude, and achievement. In *Studying teaching*, ed. J. Raths, J. Pancella, and J. S. Van Ness, pp. 43-70. Englewood Cliffs, New Jersey: Prentice-Hall.

Good, T. L., Biddle, B. J., and Brophy, J. E. 1976. The effects of teaching: an optimistic note. *The Elementary School Journal* 76:6, pp. 365-372.

Hennings, D. 1978. *Communication in action: dynamic teaching of the language arts.* Chicago: Rand McNally College Publishing.

Lewis, R. B., and Doorlag, D. H. 1983. *Teaching special students in the mainstream.* Columbus, Ohio: Charles E. Merrill.

Lord, F. E. 1974. Categories and mainstreaming in special education: perspectives and critique. In *Exceptional children: educational resources and perspectives*, ed. S. A. Kirk and F. E. Lord, pp. 419-425. Boston: Houghton Mifflin.

Madden, N. A., and Slavin, R. E. 1982. *Effects of cooperative learning on the social acceptance of mainstreamed academically handicapped students.* Center for Social Organization of Schools: Johns Hopkins University.

Ozer, M. 1980. *Solving learning and behavior problems of children.* San Francisco: Jossey-Bass.

Slavin, R. E. 1981. Synthesis of research on cooperative learning. *Educational Leadership* 38:655-660.

Slavin, R. E., Madden, N. A., and Leavey, M. 1982. *Combining cooperative learning and individualized instruction: effects on the social acceptance, achievement, and behavior of mainstreamed students.* Center for Social Organization of Schools: Johns Hopkins University.

“What Works” with Interdisciplinary Teams

Harriet Liebow

Public school systems have been given a difficult charge: to educate all the children. The movement of rural populations to urban areas, civil rights legislation, the age extension of mandatory attendance laws, and passage of the 1975 Education for all Handicapped Children Act (Public Law 94-142) have delivered increasingly diverse populations to the public schools. It has long been the responsibility of the classroom teacher to meet individual needs in physical, affective, and cognitive development, but traditional knowledge and practice in education have not provided teachers with sufficient guidance to deal with the expanded range of student abilities, backgrounds, and needs that now confront them.

The diversity of student needs contributed significantly to the development of specialization in the teaching profession (e.g., reading teachers, special educators, diagnostic-prescriptive teachers, early childhood teachers) and accelerated the incorporation of professionals from other disciplines (e.g., psychologists, counselors, health professionals, occupational and physical therapists, speech/language pathologists) in the public school systems.

The proliferation of specialized roles to meet student needs has, however, generated problems of its own. It is often the case, for example, that the very number of specialists made available through categorical funding for various special populations results in confusion for child, teacher, and administrator. The end result is that a heterogeneous population of students and an equally heterogeneous population of service providers have presented the public education system with a major problem: how to manage heterogeneity.

The management of student heterogeneity has received considerable attention in theory and practice, but the problem of coordinating the contributions of multiple consultants and multiple service providers is less well defined, and its solutions are less well developed.

The interdisciplinary team and the collegial team of teachers (Chalfant 1979) are two of the more promising mechanisms for the planning and coordination of services. Indeed, P.L. 94-142 not only provides for the inclusion of the handicapped, a previously excluded population in many school systems, but also mandates the multidisciplinary team as the mechanism by which students are to be assessed and provided with individualized education by a variety of service providers. The regulations for implementing P.L. 94-142 lay out the requirement for a multidisciplinary team and designate the membership. While there is the implicit assumption that all the professionals know *how* and *what* to do once they sit down together, traditional team approaches to evaluation, planning, and implementation of individual education programs have not always succeeded. There is increasing recognition that teams need training in order to do their job effectively.

PROBLEMS FACED BY MULTIDISCIPLINARY TEAMS

According to the mandates of P.L. 94-142, a typical multidisciplinary team meeting takes place because someone (usually a parent or teacher) suspects that a student with academic or behavioral problems is handicapped and may require special education. One phase of the process of student assessment and special education placement involves a meeting of specialists and teachers who share their assessments with each other and with the parents. The team then makes recommendations for specific services, program modifications, and/or changes in the student's placement. This process is exemplified in the following case study.

A Traditional Team Approach to Assessment

Mark was referred to the multidisciplinary team to be evaluated and considered for special education placement. Mark was seven years old and had a history of suspensions from school for disruptive behavior. He refused to do any work in school and had no friends. He was tested by a psychologist, a special education teacher, and a speech pathologist. A medical report was submitted by a pediatric neurologist.

Mark's parents, the psychologist, two special education teachers, his second-grade classroom teacher, the speech pathologist, the principal, and a school counselor met at the evaluation meeting. Test results were reported by each evaluator. Each evaluation was presented in the technical language unique to the specialist's field of expertise:

- The neurologist's evaluation stated that Mark might be suffering from a psychomotor seizure disorder which could affect his behavior.
- The psychologist reported that results from the WISC-R suggested a learning disability. Mark's performance indicated problems in

auditory sequential memory and in arithmetic reasoning. Performance on the *Bender-Gestalt Test* yielded a maturational age below expectancy with evidence of "rotations" and "distortions." Still other tests suggested anxiety and feelings of inadequacy.

- The special education teacher stated that Mark was below grade level in spelling and reading and would require assistance in these subjects. This evaluation contradicted a statement made earlier by Mark's regular teacher that he was doing well in reading.
- The speech pathologist said Mark had articulation problems. Although his language was syntactically age-appropriate, she found it to be "primitive" and suspected he had difficulty in unstructured social situations.

Based upon the concerns of these specialists, an Individual Education Plan (IEP), as required by P.L. 94-142 was developed. The multidisciplinary team recommended special education resource room instruction, speech therapy, and counseling, in addition to regular class placement. Two goals were to be addressed by a special education teacher: increasing both Mark's visual-motor integration and his spelling skills. Two goals were to be achieved by a speech/language pathologist: increasing Mark's auditory sequential memory and his use of appropriate language in social situations. Because regular classroom instruction and counseling were not classified as special services, no goals were written to account for that part of Mark's instructional program which was the responsibility of the classroom teacher and counselor. The classroom teacher was to "keep" him for math, reading, social studies, lunch, recess, science, etc. The counselor was to see him once a week. The parents' approval was requested. Everyone agreed to the IEP, and each service provider went off with his goals and objectives, in business for himself to implement an instructional program.

As mandated by law, the team reconvened after 60 days to evaluate Mark's plan. The speech pathologist, the counselor, and Mark's special education teacher all reported that Mark was making significant progress in their specialist settings. The classroom teacher and principal, however, were still upset because of Mark's continuing refusal to do written work, his fights in the cafeteria, temper tantrums, and verbal and physical aggression toward his teacher and other children. Mark was still not functioning adequately in the total school environment, even after receiving the many specialized services provided through a multidisciplinary team assessment and instructional process. There are many reasons why Mark's plan failed.

Problems in Assessment

Many factors contributed to the failure of Mark's educational plan. By first examining the assessment process, we learn that the major sources of information were the specialists, who typically rely heavily upon test results. Traditionally, test assessments yield data which evaluators convey to a usually passive audience of teachers and parents who are seldom active participants in generating the data. These test data are almost always reported in the private, professional language of the examiners. Teachers and parents may have little understanding of how such information relates to the observable behavior of the child with whom they interact on a daily basis. To them terms such as "auditory sequential memory," "pragmatics," and "visual motor integration" are not easily related to what they know about how the student reads, writes, and talks to friends on the playground.

The tendency to use professional language not only inhibits communication, it also reinforces the status of the user. Teachers and parents tend to perceive authority in terms of professional status, which endows the judgment of medical doctors, psychologists, and therapists with greater value than the views of teachers, administrators, and parents. While personality factors can influence who speaks and who is heard, the unspoken status hierarchy tends to give greater weight to statements or assertions by specialists. Thus, parents and teachers frequently hesitate to ask questions or assert their beliefs at multidisciplinary team meetings.

Another problem with the assessment information is that each "assessment" tends to be based mainly on a single isolated performance. Examination of the test results does offer a fair picture of the student's relative strengths and weaknesses and his status in relation to the norm. What is lacking, however, is insight into how the student actually functions, how he has learned to do the things he is able to do. The test data are most useful for categorizing and labeling students, rather than for planning their educational programs.

A third problem with traditional use of the assessment data arises from the quantity of information that must be assimilated and organized by the listeners. In addition to the assumption that team members can understand one another's language, there is an assumption that they are able to take quantities of assessment information and sort it into useful categories, associating different qualities of information into patterns that reveal a profile of the student's needs. In reality, however, participants tend to be overwhelmed by the quantity and variety of information and are unable, especially during a team meeting, to sort and classify what they have heard. Each piece of information may be given equal weight or each may be weighed according to the status or personal qualities of the assessor.

Problems in Program Planning

At the planning phase, traditionally, educational goals are selected from test data in terms of deficits in discrete skills or behaviors. Each specialist assumes responsibility for one or more deficit areas, and the classroom teacher is to "keep" him the rest of the time. Yet the primary responsibility for carrying out the program belongs to teachers—trained in education, but faced with designing programs based on information which is largely derived from medical/psychological model assessments and standardized, group normed tests. What should a teacher do about teaching appropriate behavior when the inappropriate behavior may be related to psychomotor seizures? How does the classroom teacher relate auditory processing problems to basic skill development? And how much does the pyschologist know about methods, materials, and conditions of the classroom? Much less attention, if any, is paid to the teacher's knowledge of the child's performance.

Perhaps the most confounding problem of program planning is that of fragmentation of services for the child. Team members tend to use assessment information to target specific deficits and assign specialist service providers to deal with those deficits. This approach tends to treat the student as a convenient bundle of little compartments labeled attending skills, language development, number concepts and visual motor integration. However, the student's ability to attend or respond, to organize, to formulate and use basic concepts is taxed all day long, in all situations. Ideally, everyone responsible for educating the student should be able to take into account, to modify, or evaluate, with understanding of how that student learns, what impedes and what facilitates his learning.

In Mark's case the primary obstacle reported by his teacher was his behavior. Yet the behavior was shunted off to a counselor to be dealt with in isolation and was not subjected to goal development because it was not to be addressed by a special education provider. Each deficit uncovered by a test was addressed by a goal, but each service provider went off with his own goal and did not necessarily know what others would be doing during the course of a day. The problem of fragmentation is common and serious.

The classroom teacher, for example, still frustrated with Mark's behavior, was unaware that the speech pathologist was using phonemes to develop auditory sequential memory, while in the classroom he was learning other sound-symbol relationships in conjunction with the reading program. Meanwhile, the special education teacher was using yet a third phonetic approach in a multisensory phonics/handwriting/spelling program. Thus Mark, who was having difficulty in spelling, now had three times more sound-symbol relationships to learn in the course of a day than his peers who presumably had no trouble learning.

To further illustrate this problem, another child receiving special education services might be observed for 15 minutes working with a teacher on fine motor skills using stacking blocks, followed by 20 minutes with an occupational therapist working on fine-motor skills, using stacking blocks. The occupational therapist, unaware that the speech therapist had introduced only one color or one question pattern, might bombard the child with questions about many colors, using language patterns the child had not yet learned. Whereupon the child might go to the speech pathologist who was initiating language therapy with an uncooperative and confused child, who whined, and the therapist would not know that the classroom teacher had been using a concrete reinforcement system to eliminate the whining.

All of the problems above—the failure to communicate in mutually understandable language, the difficulty of managing large quantities of information, the status differences of various professionals and lay people, the difficulty of translating data based on medical model assessments to action in the educational setting, the fragmentation of services and overlap of instruction—grow out of the heterogeneity of the group that was charged with the responsibility of dealing with Mark's wide array of problems. One solution that seems to address many of the problems generated by the multiple membership team is a structured process that can be applied to assessment and program development for any kind of student.

THE "WHAT WORKS" METHOD

The "What Works" method, as adapted and modified for the multidisciplinary team, has been used to augment the evaluation and IEP development function of the team in several programs in a large suburban school system.

In the application of this variation of a problem-solving process with a multidisciplinary team, both the student and the team members are considered clients. The students have learning and/or behavioral problems and the teams have problems in generating and using mutually understandable assessment data to develop coordinated programs. The "What Works" method provides a simple structured process that actively involves all participants at all phases of the process and encourages them to act collectively rather than individually. The multidisciplinary team uses all the assessment tools (e.g., standardized as well as informal test data, observation, etc.) required by federal and state regulations for the identification of educational handicaps and to document the need for special services. In addition (particularly with complex cases, or unsuccessful programs) separate problem-solving sessions are held, involving as many of the people as possible who have direct contact with the students.

"What Works" includes five questions asked by a facilitator who is familiar with the process:

1. What are your current concerns about the student?
2. What have you seen the student do well in the area of primary concern?
3. What made it possible for the student to succeed?
4. What is the team's goal for the student?
5. What is the team's plan for achieving this goal?

The first three questions each involve three steps:

- Brainstorming and categorizing the information generated by team members (assessment data)
- Exploring for commonly occurring concerns or evidence of patterns of concern
- Selecting, by consensus, from the data generated, a concern, a strategy, or a goal

Assessment

The responses to the first three questions ("What is your current concern?" "What has the student done well in this area?" "What enabled the student to succeed?") comprise the assessment data. In eliciting the concerns of each team member the student's problems or weaknesses are revealed. When the student's accomplishments are listed, patterns of strength begin to emerge. In discussing how the student was capable of these achievements, the conditions that facilitated the student's ability to function suggest strategies that can be used to address the problem area the team identifies as a primary concern.

The language of the questions and the responses from each member of the team elicits information based on each person's experience with the student. The responses tend to be given in common social language. A teacher might report that a student could not remember directions (instead of "poor auditory retention"), could not match written letters to sounds (instead of "inability to make visual auditory associations"), or forgot how to add when he started to learn how to substract (rather than "retroactive inhibition").

Brainstorming of concerns and successes encourages active participation because each participant is able to contribute what is meaningful to him. Each team member's concerns and observations of success are held to be equally valid and are not subject to comment or judgment from the group. This principle enables the facilitator to move the discussion from one group member to the next, thereby discouraging dominance by verbal, assertive group members. Throughout this process the value of each person's contribution in developing a full picture of the student is stressed.

The relevance of information needed for program planning is controlled by the specification of "current" concerns and observations. In order to separate, as much as possible, essential background information from the school-focused planning process, information about the child's educational, medical, and social history has been shared by the team members at previous meetings. Given the special purpose of the assessment and planning process, family therapy, medical treatment, and other non-school agency interventions are context variables, and the group must guard against letting them deflect the discussion away from the immediate problem of planning for the child's daily functioning in the school setting.

The sequence of the first three questions (concerns, successes, enablers) lends organization to the data–sorting data out in a pattern of weaknesses (concerns), strengths (successes), and possible strategies (enablers). The facilitator charts the data on a chalkboard or chart paper as each participant responds, providing a visual display for all team members to examine.

What are your concerns? Because the group may be composed of anywhere from three to six or more participants, each one contributing one or more items, it is necessary to use a system that categorizes the responses to "What are your current concerns?" during the exploratory step. Moreover, the process requires common language categories that would transcend the orientations of the several disciplines (psychology, education, medicine, etc.). Given the problem-solving orientation and goals of the meeting, Frank Hewitt's six levels of learning competence (Hewitt 1967) seems to offer an appropriate organizing structure for the discussion (Figure 2.1.). Hewitt describes the competencies needed in order to succeed in school and emphasizes a "learner" orientation (as contrasted with a disability orientation) that is applicable to all children, not specifically children who are handicapped. The six learning competencies are easily related to the special orientations of the different participants. In presenting them to teachers, for example, each word is paired with a common English word or phrase: *Attention* means looking, listening, and remembering; *Response* means being able to move or write or talk to demonstrate what is known; *Order* is the ability to do things in an organized, sequential way; *Exploratory* refers to knowledge of the phys-

FIGURE 2.1. *Levels of Learning Competence (From Work of Frank Hewitt).*

In order to succeed in school, a child must:

	PSYCHOLOGICAL PROCESSES
Look and listen	*Attention* perception retention
Readily try to do things	*Response* motor verbal
Follow routines	*Order* sequence organize
	BASIC CONCEPTS
Have knowledge of the properties of the physical environment	*Exploratory* attributes categories relationships
	SOCIAL, EMOTIONAL DEVELOPMENT
Be able to adjust to the social demands of the environment and be invested in seeking the approval and avoiding the disapproval of others	*Social*
	ACADEMIC ACHIEVEMENT
Acquire skill and knowledge in language and subject matter	*Mastery*

ical properties of the environment (e.g., size, shape, color, texture, time, and space); the *Social* level encompasses the area of acceptable behavior and the student's investment in desiring approval and avoiding disapproval; *Mastery* of subject matter and academic skills is understood as the goal of schooling.

For psychologists and special educators these categories are related to the psychological processes, basic concept formation, social and emotional development, and educational achievement (Figure 2.1.). This framework is used selectively in team problem solving, such as when the brainstorming produces too much data to be organized by a simple grouping procedure. For example, of six brainstormed items, four concerns might relate to "acting-out" behavior, one to slow academic achievement, and one to poor articulation. In this, team members would probably agree to focus on behavior as the primary concern. If there is no clear-cut primary concern, the team is directed to come to some agreement about which concerns may be causal in relation to other concerns and then make a selection.

What has the student done well? The same brainstorming procedure is followed with the second question "What can the student do well in the selected problem area?" This question is particularly useful because it helps team members focus on strengths. People who have been struggling with a difficult student over a period of time tend to have extremely negative perceptions of the student, losing sight of that child's strengths. The attempt to respond to this question triggers recognition of the child's positive traits or abilities. Many times team members are stymied and unable to respond, but a little prodding helps the recall of even seemingly trivial events: "He dictated a language experience story that made sense," or "She wrote two sentences on her own."

The exploration step of the second question establishes the circumstances or conditions surrounding the observed success. "What was the story about?" "Who picked the topic?" "What usually happens when he does a language experience story?" "Who else was in the group?"

The description of the task and conditions under which the child succeeded are particularly valuable in enabling participants to make associations and see causal relationships on their own, laying the groundwork for the third question.

What made it possible for the student to succeed? The first step is to review each reported success and its surrounding circumstances. The group speculates about the student's performance in relation to the conditions. If, on the day Mary wrote two sentences on her own, she had first arranged word cards into sentences and then copied them on paper, was she able to construct sentences in writing because of the way the task was broken into a two-step process? As other successes are reviewed, a pattern of conditions emerges, leading the team to find that many of Mary's successes seemed to be dependent on the teacher breaking a task into smaller steps. The "hows" and "whys" have the potential for disclosing the learning style of the child and helping to develop the strategies that might be used to implement a plan.

For instance, Kevin, an emotionally disturbed 12-year-old, was a source of constant disruption in the resource room where he received individual instruction. After a team problem-solving session, members concluded Kevin functioned better in groups than in individual sessions. Academic instruction was tried in small groups, and Kevin's disruptive behavior significantly decreased.

The team considering Kevin had developed a hypothesis and tested it. For teachers this aspect of the problem solving process may lead many times to the realization that they are drawing on their own knowledge of teaching and analytical skills. Over time, these experiences may help teachers become more aware and more confident of their own skill and knowledge.

With the assessment and analysis of the data completed, the next step in the "What Works" method is planning. The first task is to develop a goal that grows out of a primary concern or category of concerns as they were revealed in the previous steps.

What is the goal? The primary concern, sometimes simply the most frequently occurring one, is the problem to be dealt with at the first planning session. The problem is restated as a goal. If Kevin, in the previous example, did not finish any seat work, the goal is to decrease the number of tantrums, thereby increasing the amount of seat work. The criteria by which the achievement of the goal is evaluated are established in light of what is known about the student's strengths and weaknesses. Kevin had completed very few written assignments, so the evaluation criteria needed to be reasonable and the conditions under which they were to be achieved clarified. Kevin would complete one math and one written language assignment daily. The assignments would be presented in simplified sequential steps. Kevin's tantrums occurred daily, so the team decided that 4 out of 5 tantrum-free days each week for one month would be a success.

What is the plan for achieving the goal? The responses to this final question represent the synthesis of assessment, analysis, and goal setting into a plan. The student's problem and goal have been identified (questions 1 and 4); the strategies for solving the problem have been identified (questions 2 and 3). The multidisciplinary team then reviews, with each service provider, the central problem as it might be manifested at each person's point of contact with the child. The parents, when present, are considered service providers and use the team's support to clarify their roles in the home setting.

An additional strategy, the Daily Plan (Figure 2.2.), assists in explicitly working out the details of each service provider's role and responsibilities. The Daily Plan is a schedule that is filled out at the team meeting. In the process of completing it, each person who has responsibility for the child (e.g., classroom teacher, physical education teacher, music teacher, counselor, speech therapist, lunchroom supervisor, etc.) is able to discuss how the goal is to be addressed during the contact with the student. It is an opportunity to clarify details, ask for ideas, and talk about the application of strategies in specific settings.

The product of this meeting is a coordinated program, implemented by the professionals and parents with a common understanding of the student and with a joint commitment to achieving a goal. After a designated trial period, the team reconvenes to evaluate the efficacy of the plan and select a new goal.

FIGURE 2.2. *Daily Plan Form.*

DAILY PLAN

(This format may be used for planning and implementation of the instructional program. It may assist at team meetings to clarify the joint responsibilities of all persons involved in a student's program. It accounts for the child's total school day.)

Time/Period	**Activity**	**Purpose (As Related to Goals & Objectives)**	**Person Responsible**	**Environment**

A New Look at Mark: "What Works" in Action

Seven-year-old Mark, whose program was not working despite the services of a regular education teacher, special education teacher, speech pathologist, crisis resource teacher, and counselor, had become a source of increasing frustration to parents and teachers. His IEP was technically in order insofar as it showed that all primary instructional problems were being addressed by qualified professionals. He was spending maximum time in the mainstream; modifications had been tried with more or less time in special education. But Mark's behavior was still not in control, and he was losing ground academically. The multidisciplinary team reconvened. If the team was unable to reduce Mark's disruptive behavior with the resources available to them, Mark would have to be moved to a more restrictive setting, farther from home, and away from contact with a normal peer population. The team agreed to try "What Works" to revise Mark's plan of instruction.

The team consisted of a facilitator, with knowledge of the "What Works" method, and as before, the second grade classroom teacher, the special education teacher, a crisis resource teacher (CRT), the speech pathologist, the counselor, and the school psychologist.

1. *What is your current concern about Mark?*

   – Brainstorming

Sp Ed Tchr:	He elects not to work. He isn't verbal in social situations.
Cl Tchr:	He's disruptive in class.
CRT:	He has to be removed from the classroom too often.
Cl Tchr:	He's not working. He won't put anything on paper.
Sp Ed Tchr:	He's out of control in all areas of the building.
Psych:	His seizure history may be distracting us from dealing with his problems in school.
Cl Tchr:	He's aggressive with other kids.

   The team was asked to scan the list of concerns. Their responses were immediate, and it was unnecessary to categorize the responses to aid the team's selection. The following are representative samples of the exploration and selection phases.

   – Exploration

Psych:	We need to work on his behavior. Five out of eight concerns deal with his behavior.
Sp Ed Tchr:	We can't get to the academics until we deal with the behavior. When I said, "He *elects* not to work," I meant that he could do the work, but he chooses not to.
Spch Path:	He won't respond to a lot of talking, but I believe he knows exactly what I'm saying.

– Selection

Facil:	The team seems to agree that we need to focus on his behavior.
Cl Tchr:	How do I get him to behave, if he doesn't have anything to do?

The classroom teacher had begun to broach an issue that was her primary concern in working out a program. The team was able to reassure her that the specifics of Mark's program would be dealt with when his Daily Plan was discussed.

2. *What has Mark done well?* The group was silent when the second question was posed, unable to move past their frustration with Mark. The facilitator asked them to think of any small instance of appropriate behavior, in any situation. The classroom teacher was the first to respond.

– Brainstorming

Cl Tchr:	He completed an art project successfully, and he was quiet and concentrating for 40 minutes.
Spch Path:	He sat with me for one and a half hours when I was testing. He did everything I asked very pleasantly.
Psych:	He really was cooperative during my test session.
CRT:	When I get to the classroom to remove him, he is sitting like an angel, in control, with his hands folded.
Cl Tchr:	After I call for George *(the CRT)* because Mark's been acting up, Mark can settle right down just before George's hand is on the door knob. He knows exactly how long it takes George to get there.
Cl Tchr:	He sits and reads independently with good concentration but at inappropriate times.
CRT:	He interacted well with the children at recess.
Cl Tchr:	During the art project, too.
Sp Ed Tchr:	The other day during spelling, I gave him two choices of how he could do his work. He chose the first alternative and completed the task in a reasonable amount of time.

It is interesting to note that the psychologist made significantly fewer contributions than the teachers, nor did anyone use technical language.

– Exploration

During the exploration phase, the team discussed each success and the conditions surrounding the incident reported.

- He *chose* the art project. It was a *very structured project* with directions that children could follow on their own.
- During the speech testing, Mark was *alone with the speech pathologist, as he was with the psychologist.*
- The classroom teacher and the CRT had decided that when Mark's behavior was disrupting the class, the classroom teacher would signal the office, and the CRT would take Mark to a time-out room where he would stay until his tantrum was over. He would calm down as soon as the CRT was sent for, then be removed from the class for 10 minutes, and return to repeat the cycle.

– Selection

The team decided that a *structured plan* and *Mark's choice* of behavior (volitional) were significant factors in Mark's ability to manage his own behavior. With respect to the reading, it's true Mark read his library book when he was supposed to be doing seatwork, but he *reads well* and *enjoys* it. He *likes* recess, too.

3. *What made it possible for him to succeed?* The circumstances where Mark was successful were reviewed, and common characteristics were found in situations in which he performed well.

– Brainstorming

Cl Tchr: He behaves himself when he sees something is *fun* like recess and art and reading.

Cl Tchr: I think he likes *attention*. He was OK with Anne *(psychologist)* and Theresa *(speech pathologist)* because he had all their attention.

Psych: Why do you think he calms down so quickly when George *(CRT)* goes to get him?

Sp Ed Tchr: I think he knows exactly what will happen, but he's testing to see if he can change the outcome.

Spch Path: The way the testing situation is structured, he's told what to expect; he gets to practice and then he does it, so he always knows what's coming, what he's expected to do.

– Exploration

In exploring the "whys" of Mark's success in the circumstances described, the team saw a pattern. Mark performed tasks when he could anticipate what was coming, when he understood the structure and when he knew the consequences of his behavior. The team decided that he was capable of controlling himself under certain circumstances. For example, he responded well in situations where he could make choices (exert control) and when he perceived an activity to be rewarding, sometimes for the intrinsic reward (art, reading, recess) and sometimes for the attention (testing).

– Selection

Several significant factors for success were selected. Mark will control himself when he:

Knows what's expected
Knows the consequences
Can make choices
Receives attention
Perceives an activity to be fun

4. *What do we want to happen (goal)?* At this stage the team returned to the concern chosen in question 1, Mark's behavior. The goal was to increase appropriate classroom behavior. The goal was to be reached in three stages: by decreasing aggressive behavior; by increasing time spent in the learning environment; and by increasing his participation in group activities. While academic and language instruction would continue, it was recognized that expectations for the quantity and quality of academic growth would be suspended until Mark's behavior was under control, and he was really available for instruction.

5. *What is the plan for achieving the goal?* At this point the team realized that Mark's earlier plan had been importantly influenced by medical reports of a possible seizure disorder which might be affecting his behavior. In the assessment data generated during the team "What Works" session, no one reported evidence of seizures. The team felt Mark's behavior was directly linked to the circumstances in which these behaviors occurred.

   The new plan developed for Mark used as strategies the conditions and consequences (responses to question 3) which seemed to have enabled him to perform well before. These strategies were:

   - Be sure he knows what behavior is expected in each setting.
   - Be sure he knows the consequences for behaving appropriately and inappropriately.
   - Build in an element of choice so that he feels he has some control over events.
   - Use individual attention and fun activities as rewards for choosing to behave appropriately.

   These strategies would be applied to Mark's daily situations. A contract was devised to account for Mark's entire day, including follow-through at home in administering strategies (positive and negative). A reward system was used to allow Mark to earn points from each teacher for remaining in his seat, following directions, and participating in group activities to the extent each teacher specified. The positive consequences for earning an established number of points was the choice of an activity from a menu of rewards, paired with attention from the CRT (e.g., George might read with Mark, play a game of basketball, talk, go to the greenhouse, etc.). The negative consequences, immediately following each breach of contract (e.g., refusing to stay in his seat, follow a direction, etc.), were a succession of increasingly serious steps of removal—from classroom, from time-out room, from school—if violations continued. Mark's parents and teachers worked out details of follow-up at home. Each teacher had the same plan. Mark knew the plan, the expectations, and the consequences. He was allowed to make choices and was rewarded with high interest activities and attention.

The Daily Plan form (Figure 2.3.) was then developed as a culmination of the meeting, enabling each teacher to ask questions about the implications for his/her own situation and reconfirming the program. It was at this point that the classroom teacher was able to work through *her* concerns in the team meeting. She needed to have a clear and concrete idea of what Mark would be doing during handwriting. Should he be expected to write or do anything he chose? How would she explain this plan to the 28 other students in the room? The team explored with her the exact conditions—no art, no reading—yes, paper and pencil—no expectations for what gets on the piece of paper. The teacher knows now what she'll do: "I'll tell him to stay in his seat, have a pencil and paper out. I won't make him write the letters. If he gets out of his seat or refuses to take out pencil and paper, I call George. If he does follow those two directions for the 20 minutes, I give him four points." What about learning to write? The psychologist intervened with, "You're rushing him. In two weeks we'll see how the plan is working, and if it works we may build in a new set of expectations."

By planning together the specific details of Mark's program, each team member learned more about Mark and how his problems affected his functioning during physical education, handwriting, social studies, music, and all the other daily activities. The fact that he had a perceptual-motor integration problem was important, but while the behavior was being brought under control, there was to be limited pressure to tax that mode of response except during remedial training periods. By the time the planning session was over, all team members had some agreed-upon understanding of how Mark functioned and how to help him function better. Mark's psychosocial development was not relegated to the counseling room; it was now everyone's focus of attention.

No one was just "keeping" Mark any longer.

Mark—A Postscript

Mark's parents were not at the session just described because it was the team's first introduction to the "What Works" method. The plan developed was reviewed with them, and they modified and extended the plan after it was explained to them. For example, Mark's parents suggested an extension of the step-by-step removal system if his inappropriate behavior escalated. This revised plan called for his removal from classroom to time-out room, removal from time-out room to principal's office, and removal from principal's office to Mark's home by taxicab. The parents also suggested that Mark should pay the cab fare because that would be a meaningful consequence to him.

The team was prepared for Mark to test the limits of his contract, and he did. On the first day, a series of screaming tantrums led to his being sent home and a $14 cab fare. When Mark returned to school the following day, he created a scene in the classroom, then screamed as he was escorted down the hall to the principal's office by the CRT. In front of the principal's office Mark suddenly stopped screaming. "I can't afford it!" he said. Mark tested his other teachers, but within two weeks his angry and aggressive behavior was indistinguishable from that of the others in his class. New goals were set, dealing with academics and independent written work. Special interventions were gradually withdrawn; by the time Mark was a fourth grader, the bulk of the teaching responsibility was passed to the classroom teacher with continued consultation from the team.

FIGURE 2.3. *Completed Daily Plan Form for Mark.*

DAILY PLAN

(This format may be used for planning and implementation of the instructional program. It may assist at team meetings to clarify the joint responsibilities of all persons involved in a student's program. It accounts for the child's total school day.)

Time/Period	Activity	Purpose (As Related to Goals & Objectives)	Person Responsible	Environment
8:00	Opening Exercises	Follow direction–group participation	Classroom Teacher	Classroom
8:15	Hand-writing	Perceptual-Motor Development	Resource Teacher	Resource Room
8:45	Reading	Follow teacher direction–group participation for directed reading–have appropriate materials out during follow-up–attempt 10% completion of task–with option to request help from special education teacher.	Classroom Teacher	Classroom
9:30	Specials	Follow directions–participate with group	PE/Music Teacher	Specials Room
10:00	Language	Follow directions–have material out–request special education teacher assistance for written work	Classroom Teacher	Classroom

10:45	Reward Time	Choose from menu of rewards with Crisis Resource Teacher (CRT)	CRT	Resource Room
11:00	Lunch	Follow directions	Teacher On Duty	Lunchroom
11:30	Recess	Group participation or time-out depending on lunch time behavior	Teacher On Duty or CRT	
12:00	Language	Follow directions–increase verbal expression, vocabulary, language skills	Speech Pathologist	Speech Room
12:30	Math	Follow directions–complete designated assignments on specially designed papers	Classroom Teacher or CRT	Classroom
1:15	Social Studies, Sci-Art	Follow directions–passive participation acceptable	Classroom Teacher	Classroom
2:00	Reward Time	See above	CRT	Resource Room

OTHER USES OF "WHAT WORKS" BY TEAMS

The Informal Teaching Team Meeting

Peter was a third grader who had repeated a grade. For the last two school years he had been in a self-contained learning disabilities class. Here Peter had made little academic progress even though he tried very hard and had been shown by psychological tests to have above average intelligence. He was discouraged and began to retreat from contact with his classmates in the special education class; his classmates were all younger and of more limited intellectual capacity.

At a special education placement review meeting, the team decided to place Peter in a general education third-grade classroom to help his self-concept, provide contact with his normal peers, and expose him to the more stimulating content of the regular curriculum. A new psychological assessment was done to provide current information for the development of Peter's instructional plan. The assessment data indicated that Peter was weak in perceptual analysis, perceptual-motor integration, symbol learning, short-term auditory memory, and self-concept. His strengths were in social reasoning, verbal abstract reasoning, and attention to detail.

An IEP was developed which designated special education instruction in the perceptual areas and in phonics. Because the general education classroom had a reading group at his achievement level that was being taught with multisensory techniques (appropriate for him), Peter was to receive reading instruction there. He was also to participate in the rest of the general education program.

At the 60-day review meeting (mandated by P.L. 94-142) regular and special education teachers concluded that Peter was not making progress. In reading he still confused sound-symbol relationships. Peter's math program was at a standstill because he seemed unable to memorize multiplication tables.

Peter's lack of progress made the teachers feel inadequate. They said that Peter was someone "special" who required alternative teaching strategies that were beyond their level of expertise. The teachers had attempted to use the data from the psychological evaluation to construct a program. They could not translate the strengths and weaknesses described by the test data into instructional strategies. How are these strengths and weaknesses related to learning to read and do arithmetic? How does one put a weakness in symbol learning together with a strength in attending to visual detail? How does one reconcile strength in reasoning with poor math skills?

If the psychologist had explained the nature of the tasks on the tests so that the teachers could see the connection between the test performance and skills required to read and do arithmetic, the teachers might then have been able to make good use of the test information. The teaching team needed data reported in the language of teaching reading, writing, and arithmetic that would help them determine how to teach Peter.

A problem solving meeting was held to redesign Peter's program. The meeting was attended by the two classroom teachers, the special education teacher and a facilitator.

The Team Meeting

1. *What are your current concerns about Peter?*

   – Brainstorming

Tchr A:	Peter doesn't seem to remember things.
Tchr B:	Peter doesn't remember his multiplication facts.
Tchr A:	Peter can't seem to remember simple word families.
Sp Ed Tchr:	He still can't sequence sounds.
Tchr A:	He writes letters in any old order when we have spelling.
Tchr B:	He doesn't try any more.
Sp Ed Tchr:	Peter's handwriting is so poor, it's illegible.
Tchr B:	He stays away from the kids and seems to be very depressed.

   – Exploration

   Using Hewitt's levels of learning competence (Figure 2.1.), the team found that most of its concerns were related both to attention (perception and retention) and to response and order (motor and verbal response in an organized, sequential manner).

   Their concerns were in fact comparable to the weaknesses diagnosed by the psychological evaluation. The categories were now much broader, but they were more meaningful to teachers because they were educational. Peter had trouble remembering words and math facts; he could not easily go from the symbol to the sound or reproduce them in sequence; he could not remember the visual sequence of symbols to spell, and he had trouble forming letters.

   – Selection

   The team agreed that the categories of concern–attention, response, and order–were interrelated and they selected as their primary concern Peter's inability to remember symbols and facts in sequential order. One concern, Peter's social and emotional functioning, was informally addressed by team members, but they hypothesized that this was a result, rather than a cause, of Peter's academic failure.

2. *What has Peter done well?*

   – Brainstorming

Tchr A:	Peter remembered the landforms and found them on a map.
Sp Ed Tchr:	He did well on a spelling test, recently.
Tchr B:	He completed a multiplication paper on his own, correctly.
Tchr A:	Peter named all the continents.

– Exploration

As the team surveyed Peter's successes, they remarked on the seemingly contradictory evidence of Peter's ability to remember and to sequence steps in computation when memory was such a primary concern. Each team member described the circumstances surrounding Peter's successful performances. The social studies lesson landforms had included maps, pictures, and labeled overheads; Peter seemed to be very interested in the subject matter and was unusually attentive. The math assignment was done in an aide's room where there were charts illustrating the sequence of steps in multiplying; Peter used them as a reference and seemed to remember the facts without using drawings or his fingers. His spelling test had been better than previous tests he had taken. While the other students had to know more words, Peter successfully completed a contract with the teacher to learn seven words. His contract included a list of steps showing how to study the words.

3. *What made it possible for him to succeed?* The probable answers to this question were so clear to the teachers that they had no need formally to brainstorm and explore. Peter's teachers immediately offered the ideas:

Tchr A:	His own interest motivated him to learn those continents and landforms, and I just helped along by providing auditory and visual input, simultaneously.
Tchr B:	There was a chart showing the sequence of steps in multiplying that helped keep him on target. He obviously understands what it's all about or he wouldn't even be able to use the chart on different examples. Maybe without that worry of remembering the steps, he could recall the simple facts. He really can use visual aids.
Sp Ed Tchr:	When his attention is focused, he can remember. That spelling contract helped him zero-in on the task.
Tchr B:	He had another help, too. The steps were there as a reminder about how to organize his studying.
Tchr A:	He's bright and he likes getting information. He'll work on keeping his attention on interesting things.

Selection

The team selected three strategies to use with Peter: motivating him to focus his attention through high interest materials; helping him focus his attention using visual aids to supplement auditory input and aid recall; making him aware, through rules and contracts, of what and how to remember.

4. *What is the team's goal?* The team decided that its priority was to help Peter learn to compensate for his memory problem because this would assist him to improve his spelling, sight vocabulary, and mastery of math facts. Using what they knew about how he had been able to learn, they would exploit his ability to learn rules, use high interest material, combine auditory and visual input and teach him specific strategies for remembering. Their specific objectives were that Peter would (1) increase to ten the number of words he could spell correctly on a spelling test, (2) increase the number of words he could recognize from 10 to 20, and (3) complete a specified number of multiplication computations correctly.
5. *What is the team's plan?* The team discussed each class in filling out his Daily Plan, drawing upon one another's suggestions and coordinating his program with respect to content and teaching strategies. For example, in math class, Peter would use a step sequence chart until he was able to demonstrate that he could recall facts automatically. He would contract to learn one multiplication table a week, planning with his teacher the way he would practice each day. In spelling, the current approach was continued with the words taken from his word family list in reading where certain generalizations about phonics were stressed. Thus spelling words would not be an arbitrary collection of words, but would be selected around phonetic rules, capitalizing on Peter's ability to apply rules. Peter's sight vocabulary would also be structured around his own interests and combined with a contracting system and a multisensory strategy. Peter's reading program was to include a language experience component with content from his social studies and science classes. (It is noteworthy that Peter's classroom teacher decided to implement this approach with Peter's whole reading group because she saw the benefit for all of her students.) The special education teacher would complement the reading program by monitoring and reteaching selected sight vocabulary through a multi-sensory strategy. She also assumed responsibility for the written language portion of Peter's program and coordinated it, wherever possible, with reading.

   Peter's parents participated in the meeting and agreed to the plan, stating that they had gained insight into their son's problems—an insight they had not had in Peter's three years of school failure and after countless meetings. They also volunteered to dismiss his tutor who had been using still another method to teach reading to Peter and whose existence had been previously unknown to Peter's teachers.

   Participants in the reevaluation conference, two weeks after implementation, concluded that the plan was working. Two years later, Peter had made two years' growth in math (a significant increase in rate of learning compared to Peter's 1.9 years' growth

> in the previous three years), 2.4 years' growth in reading, and 1.5 years' in spelling. His fund of general information showed four years of growth. Peter's report card became a source of pride to him. While Peter's learning disabilities did not go away, he seemed to have learned sufficient compensatory strategies to allow him to function and feel good about himself. The teachers, too, had learned something about themselves as they made adjustments in their programs for Peter. While they previously thought themselves incapable of working with a student experiencing as many problems as Peter, they now believed they were able to work effectively with a wider range of learning problems.

Peter, like Mark, is typical of many students. Teachers tend to say, "They need something else besides the regular classroom." In fact, these teachers may have the skills and knowledge to meet such students' needs, but may be unable to apply them for lack of a systematic approach to problem solving. The "What Works" method provides a structure for working with students who experience a variety of learning or behavior problems, a tool for the multidisciplinary and teaching teams that must address these problems.

Using "What Works" in Other Educational Settings

The "What Works" method has also been used successfully in other educational settings with students who are more severely handicapped. In one instance a principal wanted to assist a team of therapists and teachers of the severely and profoundly handicapped. The principal's interest was to encourage teachers and specialists who worked with the same child to value each other's perceptions and skills and use each other as resources. A facilitator, familiar with the "What Works" method, but not trained in working with profoundly retarded children, was able to help the team arrive at a primary concern and discover strengths in a child who had almost no communication abilities and limited awareness of external stimuli. Their primary focus, growing out of the brainstorming, exploration, and selection of concerns, was getting the child to notice and respond to stimuli presented by the teachers. The child's only response seemed to be to things that made noises—crunchy food, the thwack of a basketball, sound through earphones. Each person who worked with the child had some confirming experiences, but they had not brought together their knowledge to allow them to see a pattern; each had worked with the child in isolation, each carrying out his own program. Understanding the child's responses to noise, they were able to help one another identify a specific way in which each teacher could use noise as a reward for attending to the teacher. The facilitator had only to structure the process of identification of concerns, successes, and strategies. The teachers used their own data to develop a plan.

In a regular school that had a number of mainstreamed emotionally impaired youngsters, "What Works" was used to plan programs for them. In this case the "What Works" method was used to deal with the complex individual needs of students for whom, because they had encountered so much failure and rejection in other settings, it was critical to build initial no-fail experiences. The "What Works" method helped the staff gain adequate understanding of the students and coordinate their efforts around common goals. It also made it possible for the staff to monitor and control their own responses to the students so that the students would experience maximum consistency from the significant adults in the environment. A new principal was assigned to the school after the "What Works" method had been in use for some time. Team members were apprehensive at first about the principal's reaction to the use of this approach to the development of individual plans. With a team consisting of one or two classroom teachers, two special education teachers, an aide, a psychologist, a counselor, a reading teacher, a speech pathologist, sometimes a music and a physical education teacher, a pupil personnel worker, and a representative of the special education administrative office, it often required two hours to develop a program. The team worried that the new principal would compute the dollar cost of two hours of that much professional time and decide that it was impractical to continue approaching each case that way. After observing the use of "What Works" by the multidisciplinary team, she finally offered her opinion of the system in the form of a question: "Why don't we use this process with normal children? After all, the 'disturbed' children seem to be doing better now than those who have only been identified as having behavior problems!" Apparently the principal perceived the process to be worth the initial investment of time, especially if one compared this time to the cumulative hours it took to deal with problem children in constant repetitive, ineffective cycles.

CONCLUSION

As the criteria for school services become more limiting, the definition of "normal" will expand. Some of the programs for the more mildly handicapped may disappear from the school system, but most of the students will not; only their labels will disappear. Other students with special needs—the disadvantaged, the culturally different, the non-English speakers, those from mobile or unstable families—will also remain. Thus, teachers will have even greater need for specialist and collegial support teams to help solve students' problems. And in fact, the multidisciplinary team is, by law, a fact of school life. As demonstrated in this chapter, the "What Works" method offers a unified instructional approach to these teams, an approach that can be adapted to a wide range of students' needs.

REFERENCES

Chalfant, J. C., Pysh, M., and Moultrie, R. 1979. Teacher assistance teams: a model for within–building problem solving. *Learning Disability Quarterly* 2:85-96.

Hewitt, F. M., with Forness, S. R. 1967. *Education of exceptional learners.* Boston: Allyn and Bacon.

Ozer, M. N. 1980. *Solving learning and behavior problems of children.* San Francisco: Jossey-Bass.

Reynolds, M. C., 1979. Interpreting Public Law 94-142. In *The most enabling environment: education is for all children*, ed. S. Sunderlin, pp. 19-26. Washington, D. C.: Association for Childhood Education International.

Sarason, S. B. 1982. *The culture of the school and the problem of change.* Boston: Allyn and Bacon.

Transferring "What Works" to the Regular Classroom

Ruth Harris

Instruction in a specialized setting for a portion of each school day may be the most appropriate educational arrangement for students who need individual attention, those who do not require major changes in the regular curriculum. Too often, however, students are removed from the regular classroom with little or no coordination between the regular teacher and specialist regarding the instructional approach to be used, the material to be taught, and the objectives to be achieved. Furthermore, when segregated instruction is provided without efforts to transfer student accomplishments to the regular setting, the improvement over the long run is minimal (Jenkins, Barksdale, and Clifton 1978; Rose, Lessen, and Gottlieb 1982). There is no guarantee that achievement that occurs in the specialized setting will translate into gains in other settings. Any individualized help, to be worthwhile, must include assistance that enables the student experiencing problems to demonstrate continued gains in the regular classroom.

The "What Works" method facilitates the generalization of academic and behavioral learning gains from an individual or small group setting to a less restrictive instructional environment such as the regular classroom. It does this by helping students to become more aware of their own successful learning strategies. Through the questions and interactive dialogue of the method, the educational specialist facilitates the student's conscious awareness of positive behaviors, raises this consciousness to the level of verbalization, and helps to transfer and apply these strategies to a wider array of learning situations. Thus, the student becomes a carrier of information about how he learns. The emphasis is on "process"–how the student learns–rather than on "product"–what the student learns.

Using the "What Works" method, the specialist creates an environment where conspicuous learning takes place. Through consciousness-raising and reinforced dialogue, the student experiences a learning awareness on a daily basis that can be communicated freely with teachers, parents, and others. The dialogue that follows illustrates the many benefits of this communication:

Cl Tchr: What did you do in Miss Jones' remedial reading class today?

Student: I got to play a game because I had three stars on my "What Works" list. *(Handing the list to the teacher.)* I even won a sticker.

Cl Tchr: *(Looking at the list.)* I see that you have three stars next to "I need to move a marker across the words so I can read them in the right order."

Student: Yes, the marker really helps me. Otherwise I skip words or read them all mixed up. Would it be all right if I use a marker when I read in your classes, too?

A second dialogue illustrates that this knowledge about learning strategies can be transferred and reinforced across subject areas as well. For example:

Read Tchr: John, you really have improved in your reading. You are reading so much more smoothly now. How is your reading going in the classroom?

John: Better, but my math isn't so good. I got five wrong today. I get the numbers all mixed up when I copy them from my book.

Read Tchr: You mean that when you copy the problems from your math book, you write down the wrong numbers?

John: Yes.

Read Tchr: John, that sounds like the difficulty you had mixing up the order of the words when you read. What worked for you to read the words in order?

John: It helped when I moved a marker across the words so I could read them in the right order.

Read Tchr: That's right, John. It helped when you moved a marker across the words so you could read them in the right order. What do you think would help you to copy numbers in the right order?

John: Use a marker?

Read Tchr: That's a good idea, John, to use a marker to move across the numbers in the math problems as you copy them. Let's try it and see if it works. What kind of math problems are you working on now?

John: We're subtracting with three numbers.

Read Tchr: Okay, John, I'll write some subtraction problems on a sheet of paper, and then you can copy them just as you do from your math book. Only, what are you going to try new today?

John: I'll move a marker across the numbers as I copy them.

This illustration of transfer is significant because the more applicable a learning strategy is to other experiences, the more widespread is the student's success.

"WHAT WORKS" TO DEVELOP LEARNING SKILLS

The "What Works" method is a problem-solving dialogue first used between the specialist, teacher, or parent, and the student to identify learning problems. Gradually the dialogue becomes internalized, and the student learns to use it without assistance from others. This dialogue includes five basic questions. These questions may be developed in a variety of ways as the specialist draws from students their own concerns, their own successful strategies based upon past achievements, and their own plans for using these strategies to solve current problems.

There are three important classroom outcomes of using the "What Works" method with problem learners in specialist settings, outcomes that increase the student's ability to transfer learning to the regular classroom.

Students Learn to Communicate Needs

"How do you do this? I don't get it!" are statements commonly heard both in the classroom and in the specialist setting. The "What Works" dialogue can be used to help students specify more clearly the information they need. "How do you do this?" can be clarified as a more specific need by the specialist who responds, "What is it that you don't get?" The specialist's response corresponds to the first of the five basic "What Works" questions, "What is your concern at this time?" If a student says, "Long division," the specialist may say, "What step in this long division problem is most difficult for you?" This interaction continues until the student is able to clarify exactly which step is most problematic and can ask, "Will you tell me how to figure out how many times the outside number goes into the first part of the inside number?"

If the student persists in making general statements (for example, indicating he doesn't understand any of the problem), then it is useful to help him to specify what parts he already knows by asking, "What part of this problem do you understand?" or "Show me what you can do." This response on the part of the teacher corresponds to the second dialogue question. In this way the specialist demonstrates that the student does, indeed, "get" some of it. The specialist can help them model (through the use of examples) questions that are more specific requests.

As students learn and practice asking questions with more specificity, they become more in charge of their learning, clarify their thinking, and narrow their concern to the boundaries of the problem areas. Thus, the student experiencing difficulty with the division problem no longer feels himself to be completely incapable at math. The student recognizes that he can do most of the problem but needs help on one specific part. As interactions with the specialist become more specific, students are better able to receive the help required and are more likely to interact in a positive manner with specialists who provide assistance.

In this way, the "What Works" method is a means of achieving more efficient use of classroom time. For example, suppose a teacher has just assigned tasks to groups of students in the classroom. As the teacher sits down to work with one group, hands spring up from several students in other groups. She decides to spend a few minutes answering questions before focusing on one of the groups. Typical student responses include, "I don't get it," "I don't know how to do it," "What do I do?" These nonspecific queries do nothing to enhance a teacher's willingness to respond at length, since a teacher is likely to believe she has already explained what is expected of her students. Imagine next a student who poses a question in a more specific format. "I understand what to do when there is a zero in the one's place, but I need help on figuring out this problem where there are zeros in the ten's and one's place" or "Could you tell me how to pronounce the third syllable in this word?" or "Will you check this problem before I do the others to see if I am doing this the right way?"

Specific, concrete questions about areas of concern are seldom generated spontaneously from students. Teaching students to be specific about what they need takes time, but the time gained and the frustration avoided make this effort well worthwhile.

Students Develop a Positive Approach to Learning

Using the "What Works" method, the educational specialist may observe the student making a correct response and share that information with the child. In this way she is assisting the child to answer the second question of the "What Works" dialogue, "What have you been able to do successfully?" The specialist then follows this interaction with the third dialogue question by asking, "What worked?" or "How were you able to get that right?" At this point she uses the student's description of what worked for him and "feeds" it back to him verbally using his words and using the pronouns "you" or "yours." For example, "That's a good idea of yours to say the letters as you write them. That worked for you."

By using a personalized repetition, the specialist reinforces the "ownership" of the strategy that worked for the student. This ownership is further enhanced when the student is asked the question, "What was it that worked for you? Can you tell me again?" The student restates the strategy, thus clarifying it and personalizing it with the pronouns "I" and "me." "It helps me when I say the letters." As an additional reinforcement, the student may write down the strategy so that he has a written record of what works for him stated in his own words.

It is important that throughout this process the educational specialist be responsive to the ideas presented by the student. This open attitude creates an environment receptive to a student's ideas, and it increases the student's awareness of his own competencies as they contribute these ideas. A student thereby feels better about learning.

The specialist can also include in the "What Works" dialogue observations about how the student learns. For example: "It seems as though it helps you to copy correctly when you copy three letters at a time. Would you be willing to try that on the next sentence?" or "Sometimes it helps students to remember right and left when they think of which hand they write with. Would you be willing to try that? Would that be OK with you? What are you going to think of in order to remember right and left?"

In each of these interactions the specialist actually solicits a verbal agreement with the student about a strategy that works. This verbal agreement reinforces the open interaction between teacher and student and highlights the student's knowledge of what learning strategies work for him. He now has a conscious awareness of successful strategies that can be used in other settings. Again, as a result of focusing on what works for him, a student develops a more positive approach to learning.

Students Become More Independent Learners

Teachers admire "independent" learners. At the same time, educators do not demonstrate a concerted effort to develop strategies that teach children this skill. Rather, independence is a hoped-for by-product of our educational system. The "What Works" method fosters independent learning in a planned, systematic way.

A specialist may decide, for example, that "John is a kinesthetic learner. I will have him trace words when he has trouble." Perhaps this works very well when the teacher asks him to trace the word. However, John is still dependent on someone else's direction in how to approach a learning task. Instead of merely praising a student for learning a task, or for successfully using techniques that she suggests, a teacher might begin a dialogue with the student about what helps him solve problems. For example, the teacher might say, "Good, John. Your having a chance to trace the letters worked for you. Don't you think?" John is thus encouraged to respond, "Yes, it helps me when I trace the letters." The teacher continues the dialogue and attempts in other ways to make the idea as clear as possible to John. For example, one response might be, "That's a good idea, John, for you to trace the letters. Now why don't you write it down?"

It is useful for a student to maintain a list of strategies that work for him. The teacher can use this list to review with the student those learning strategies which have been successful in the past. Copies of this list can be made for the student to tape to his desk, take to his other classes, and bring home. This reinforces the student's own knowledge of learning techniques and assists with the transfer of strategies learned in the specialist setting to other learning environments.

As problem learners develop more control over their own learning by focusing on strategies that work for them, they begin to know what is needed for them to be successful on particular tasks. The third and fourth dialogue questions ask a student to consider, "What goal would you like to achieve with this problem?" and "What is your plan to achieve this goal?" As a result, increasing responsibility for learning is shifted from educators to students. Also, in achieving this shift, the responsibility for raising a student's awareness of his ability takes on greater importance in the teaching role.

USING THE "WHAT WORKS" METHOD FOR ACADEMIC IMPROVEMENT

In addition to helping students become aware of a variety of learning strategies that can be used in different educational settings, the specialist can use the "What Works" method to develop a plan for academic improvement. The following is the story of one student who showed significant academic gains through his work with an educational specialist using this method.

A Case Study

Michael was a 13-year-old student referred to a reading specialist because of academic performance well below grade level. Specific areas of difficulty for Michael were visual motor perception, reading, math, memory skills, study skills, motivation, and self-concept. His teachers reported that, while Michael was conscientious about his work and tried to complete assignments, he did not retain material presented in class and frequently failed his assignments.

The reading specialist worked with Michael in two ways. First, she provided him with daily one-to-one instruction for six weeks. Second, she communicated closely with Michael's teachers to increase the probability that learning would carry over into the regular setting.

One-to-one instruction involved reading and other academics presented within the framework of the "What Works" method. With emphasis on the third problem-solving question ("What works?"), Michael kept a written list of strategies that worked for him in his academic problem areas. This list grew over the six-week period as Michael became aware of previously successful strategies, and as he developed new ones. Michael's goal in listing these strategies was to become more aware of what helped him learn, thus, gaining more control and flexibility over his own learning.

The following strategies were listed by Michael over the six-week period:

1. Check my own work first before handing it in.
2. When I am stuck, say, "Please give me a hint."
3. When I am stuck, say, "Please show it to me" or "Please show me again."
4. Say the word out loud as I look at it, or say the letters out loud as I spell it.

5. When I use words on a list to fill in blanks, cross out the ones I have used.
6. When I am stuck on a word, I could say, "Please give me one sound."
7. When I am counting items on a worksheet, cross them out as I count so that I can keep track.
8. Point with my finger as I read.
9. Put a mark on something I want to remember.
10. Go back and correct myself.
11. Remember a key word. For instance, to remember the blend "pr," remember the word "prize."
12. When something is difficult, break it into parts.
13. When I have to memorize, put things in groups.
14. Ask myself after I have read something or written an answer, "Does it make sense?"
15. Remember the magic "e" on the end of words (e.g., kit, kite).

The reading teacher used a reinforcement system to encourage Michael's awareness of successful strategies. This reinforcement was called the "star system." One star was given if Michael demonstrated a successful strategy even if he could not articulate what that strategy was. Michael's teacher increased the boy's awareness of what strategies worked for him by sharing her observations of what worked: "Michael, what seemed to help you to copy that long word from the board was that you said the letters out loud to yourself. Then you could hear them as you copied. Was that what worked for you, Michael?" The student then repeated his impression of what was said, and this statement was written down on the list and given one star.

Two stars were given if Michael could demonstrate a successful learning strategy and state what worked in his own words. This statement was written down verbatim and two stars were awarded.

Three stars were given if Michael shared spontaneously one of his successful learning strategies with another student. It is said that a true measure of learning occurs when one is able to teach another. A student's own ability to teach yields side benefits of confidence, positive peer interaction, and the growth of learning strategies that reflect the unique learning style of each student.

This three-star system is not static in that the same learning strategy that received one star yesterday can receive two or more when Michael demonstrates that he knows what worked and shares this strategy with another student. This reward system does not prevent the instructor from introducing other learning strategies, either. When a teacher introduces a learning strategy, the student has the opportunity to try it and see if it does "work." If the strategy does work, the student has the chance to make it his own by articulating how the strategy was successful. The true test of a student's responsibility for himself occurs when the student experiences difficulty on a task and is able to select a strategy from his own list of "what works" and apply it in a new situation. The significance of this "transfer" cannot be overemphasized when independent learning is the goal; therefore, if Michael encountered difficulty copying arithmetic problems accurately, and he transferred his strategy of "say it out loud as I write," applying the same strategy to numbers as he did to words, he would demonstrate true independence and responsibility for his learning.

The teacher consultant spoke often with Michael's regular teachers. They learned about how the "What Works" method was used with him and readily agreed to try the dialogue in the regular setting. As a result, when Michael experienced difficulty with a task, his regular teacher responded differently than she had in the past. Rather than saying, "Would you like me to show you how to do this?" she said, "What would help you?" When Michael did not respond readily to this question, the teacher offered options to him: "Would you like me to say it again?" "Would you like me to explain it another way?" "Would you like me to give you an example?" or "Are you concerned about the whole word or just one syllable?" Michael could then select one of the proposed strategies. These questions prompted Michael to investigate his own needs and become more specific about what would help him. As he became more discriminating, the more general question of "What works?" would then be used to generate a clear response.

Michael's parents were also encouraged to use the "What Works" method with him at home. His parents saw evidence that Michael used more conscious strategies in his homework assignments, and they noticed his pleasure in demonstrating new strategies. This resulted in reinforcement of Michael's problem-solving method in the three settings where he spent the most time during the day: his regular classroom, his reading class, and at home.

Michael showed rapid improvement in his academic work. Although the reading specialist did not work directly with him the entire academic year, she did maintain communication with his regular teachers. His teachers readily admitted that what worked for Michael was his awareness of his own learning style. This caused him to take greater responsibility for asking for the help he needed in order to complete his assignments. He maintained and memorized his own list of strategies and used them to become more independent and responsible for his learning. Two years later Michael was on grade level in his academic work.

USING THE "WHAT WORKS" METHOD FOR BEHAVIOR MANAGEMENT

The job of the specialist in behavior management is to facilitate the student's ability to identify the problem behavior as the student perceives it; to heighten the student's awareness of this identified problem and its possible solutions; and to generate problem-solving strategies to change the behavior. The ultimate goal of the "What Works" method in behavior management is to enable students to internalize the problem-solving dialogue so that they are aware of and responsible for managing their own behavior in all educational settings. Using "What Works," the specialist elicits from students some ideas about successful strategies. These strategies are more likely to be successful because the students have taken an actual part in their own problem solving and are responsible for the coping strategies (Ozer 1980).

When discipline is the issue, the effectiveness of any approach depends on the student's and teacher's perceptions of who is responsible for the problem. Sufficient time is required in the initial planning session to determine the student's perception of the problem. Only if the student "owns" the problem will he have an investment in solving it. Quite often there is a conflict between the student's perception of the problem and the specialist's, parent's, or teacher's perception of the problem. The goal is not to determine who is correct but to involve the student in planning a solution that will be satisfactory to all involved.

For example, the student who is constantly disrupting the class in order to gain attention is a problem to the teacher and the rest of the class; however, the student himself may not have a vested interest in solving his problem of "talking out of turn," or "getting out of his seat," or "throwing things around the room." To the disruptive student, this inappropriate behavior may be self-rewarding; therefore, the focus of the teacher on the student's disruptive behavior may not be as productive as attention to more acceptable behaviors that are incompatible with acting out in class. The teacher must encourage acceptable classroom behaviors so that the student can attract the attention and recognition of both the teacher and the class. To involve the disruptive student in dialogue about classroom behaviors that are appropriate is more likely to yield the desired outcome than a lecture that demands the student to remain seated or be punished.

Occasionally students are not even aware of their "problem" behaviors. For example, some students have annoying habits in class that bother only the teacher or a few other students. A case in point is Jennifer, a second-grader who constantly tapped her pencil on her desk. One day the teacher's pencil-tapping threshold was reached. She looked at Jennifer at her desk, reading avidly, to the accompaniment of tapping. "Jennifer, please stop that!" Jennifer obediently looked up from her book, still tapping her pencil. She had stopped the only activity she was aware of–reading! There was no awareness on her part that she was annoying her teacher by tapping a pencil on the desk. Teachers must communicate clearly what is bothering them if they are interested in changing student behaviors. Sometimes clear communication is all that is needed. At other times it may be necessary for the teacher and student to develop a plan that will result in classroom behavior that is satisfactory to all parties involved.

Particularly important in this use of the "What Works" dialogue for behavior management are the questions that inquire about success. These questions must be followed by very specific inquiries about who, what, when, where, and how, so that the student is able to recreate the successful experience. The specialist can also use these questions to work with the student's parents and teachers to help them to remember past successes with the problem student. Not only does this clarify circumstances surrounding positive behavior so that behavior-coping strategies can be identified, but it gives students, parents, and the teachers cause for optimism.

The following story is a case study illustrating the use of the "What Works" method in the area of behavior management.

"What Works" with Behavior Outbursts

Jess was a fourth-grade student who often lost control of his behavior. He had been known to leave his seat and attack other students, punching, jabbing, and at times pulling the chairs out from under others. He expressed no remorse after these episodes had passed. He said that he just did not know what came over him. Punishment usually took the form of removal from the classroom to the office, the hall, or even to his own home for suspension. He was also kept in from recess, denied gym (his favorite activity), and detained after school. Jess met regularly with the school psychologist and guidance counselor. Although he was above average in general ability, Jess fell behind in his work. He missed more and more classroom instruction as he was removed from the room because of his outbursts.

When Jess met with the resource teacher, the initial question "What are your concerns?" was asked. Jess was encouraged to list as many problems as he could. The resource teacher elicited at least three concerns, then encouraged Jess to identify the one that bothered him most. Jess responded by saying, "I don't like to be seen sitting out in the office or in the hall. Everyone stares at me. I want to stay in the room like everyone else." Since Jess was responsible for this concern, its resolution was in his own interest. In this situation, the teacher's expressed concern was for the safety of the children in her classroom. Unfortunately, this was not a concern of Jess.

The second step of the "What Works" method was for the resource teacher to solicit from Jess at least three occasions when he was able to "stay in the classroom like everyone else" for at least half a day. Jess recalled with difficulty three occasions. To recall positive examples of his own behavior was tantamount to a reversal in thinking for Jess. Once three occasions were mentioned by Jess, his teacher asked him to pinpoint the one that was most clear to him in his memory. "Well, I guess it was last Friday." The teacher then asked questions to sharpen Jess' memory of the day. "Was it morning or the afternoon? What were you doing? What was the rest of the class doing? Where were you sitting? What materials were you using?" Once these questions were answered, the resource teacher asked Jess what he thought worked to enable him to stay in class. Again, three examples of what worked were solicited, and he was asked to select the one that seemed most significant to him. "I think what worked the most was that we had physical education class at the beginning of the afternoon, and I didn't feel so antsy after that, so I could settle down." This was explored further with Jess, and it was agreed that physical activity seemed to dilute his aggressive behavior.

Resrce Tchr: That's a good idea of yours, Jess, to be physically active first so that you can then settle down and be allowed to stay in the classroom. Let's see if we can use your idea so that you can stay in the classroom more often this week. We only have physical education three times a week. What might you do on Tuesdays and Thursdays that would be physically active?

Jess: I could go to the gym myself and do something active.

Resrce Tchr: That's a good idea to do something active, Jess, but there wouldn't be any supervision in the gym, so it would not work for you to go to the gym alone. What physical activity do you especially enjoy? Maybe it does not have to be done in the gym.

Jess: I really like using the punching bag.

Resrce Tchr: That's a good idea of yours, Jess, to use a punching bag. Where could we put it so that it would be near your regular classroom but not disturb anyone?

Jess: How about the supply closet near the restroom?

With agreement from his regular teacher, Jess and his resource teacher looked into the feasibility of using the supply closet. With some rearranging, it worked out well. It was then agreed that Jess could use the punching bag for five to ten minutes on Tuesday and Thursday afternoon for the next week. Jess had an especially good day Tuesday and was able to stay in the regular classroom all afternoon. However, on Wednesday, by mid-morning, he seemed to be extremely anxious and restless. Noticing this, his regular teacher went over to him and asked him how he felt. "Like hitting someone," he answered. There had been close communication between Jess' classroom teacher and resource teacher, so she felt comfortable with her response:

Cl Tchr: What do you think would help, Jess?

Jess: Well, it's not Tuesday or Thursday, but could I go punch that punching bag?

Cl Tchr: Yes, Jess, that's a good idea, to punch the punching bag when you feel like hitting someone.

Jess returned ten minutes later and seemed more relaxed and ready to settle down to work. At the end of the morning, his teacher asked, "Jess, what worked for you to settle down this morning and stay in the room when you felt so restless?" Jess answered, "Punching the bag helped me to settle down."

It was then agreed that Jess would raise his hand with the special signal when he felt like striking out and he would then be excused for five or ten minutes to punch the bag.

As several weeks passed, Jess used the punching bag less frequently. He also seemed to be more aware of his feelings and their ranges of intensity. Jess became more in charge of himself, more in control. The blind rages which had led to so many unfortunate consequences dissipated. Jess achieved the goal he had set for himself, which was to stay in the regular classroom for longer periods of time so that others would not see him sitting in the hall. His classroom teacher worked with Jess to substitute other forms of energy release for his punching bag activity. With this increase in Jess' self-control, his teachers no longer viewed him as a physical threat to others.

Jess also improved his grades. In addition, other students became more accepting of him. Several students selected Jess as a partner for certain activities listed on a sociogram, whereas before the treatment he was not selected by any students as a desired partner.

CONCLUSIONS

The "What Works" method is a consciousness-raising approach to problem-solving which assists with the transfer of learning from one educational setting to another. It is process- rather than product-oriented in that "how" the student is able to succeed is emphasized as much as the achievement itself. Through dialogue, students are reponsible for generating strategies that may be applied to their problems without regard to educational setting or subject content.

REFERENCES

Hickey, K. A., Imber, S. C., and Ruggiero, E. A. 1979. Modifying reading behavior of elementary special needs children: a cooperative resource-parent program. *Journal of Learning Disabilities* 12:7, pp. 444-449.

Jenkins, J. R., Barksdale, A., and Clinton, L. 1978. Improving reading comprehension and oral reading: generalization across behaviors, settings, and time. *Journal of Learning Disabilities* 11:10, pp. 607-617.

Ozer, M. N. 1980. *Solving learning and behavior problems of children.* San Francisco: Jossey-Bass.

Rose, T. L., Lessen, E. I., and Gottlieb, J. 1982. A discussion of transfer of training in mainstreaming programs. *Journal of Learning Disabilities* 15:3, pp. 162-165.

Inservice: "What Works" with Learning Problems

Elizabeth F. Swanson, EdD / Nancy Smith, PhD

Regular teachers have always had handicapped learners in their classrooms. But today teachers work with more handicapped learners than ever before. By 1983, 4.3 million handicapped children aged three through 21 were receiving special education and related services. This amounts to over 10 percent of all students enrolled in public schools in the United States (U.S. Department of Education 1984).

At present the majority of handicapped students spend most of the school day in the regular classroom. Consequently, teachers who received little if any instruction in special education now work with problem learners every day, and often feel that they are inadequately prepared for this responsibility (Ringlaben 1981). This is unfortunate, because teacher inadequacy is not the problem that these teachers feel it to be. Researchers have found that with training in problem-solving skills and the use of a variety of strategies to reach a single instructional goal, regular teachers can become highly successful with problem students (Essexville-Hampton Public Schools 1975; Swanson 1980).

The "What Works" method differs from traditional problem-solving strategies in several ways. First, the five questions that are asked and addressed by teachers allow them not only to generate strategies for solving problems, but to determine an appropriate strategy for the teacher by focusing on previously successful methods. The question "What works?" in relation to "What is the problem?" is really asking, "What did you do in the past that succeeded with this problem?" These questions prompt teachers to draw upon their own success experiences as models for action. This brings to the problem the feelings of confidence associated with a previously successful experience. Thus, "What works?" is a pivotal question that helps the teacher to generate strategies to solve problems. It identifies those strategies most likely to work and brings into awareness a teacher's feelings about past successes.

Another characteristic of the "What Works" method which differentiates it from other problem-solving approaches is its emphasis upon the brainstorming and selecting processes. "What is the problem?" coupled with "What works?" and "What did you do in the past that succeeded with this problem?" defines the student's needs and generates strategies to meet these needs. Addressing these questions through this process of brainstorming and selecting leads to greater awareness of the student's specific problem and the teacher's most appropriate course of action. Brainstorming encourages an active, nonjudgmental search for strategies that enhance learning in each situation. It generates the required variety of strategies from which teachers can select as they define their plan of action. This process is a critical step toward a creative solution to the student's problem.

Below are descriptions of two inservice training courses that help teachers work more effectively with handicapped students in the regular classroom. Results using the "What Works" dialogue in these courses show how the regular classroom can become a setting where the problem student succeeds rather than fails. Supervised training experiences for teachers are stressed using a variety of strategies to achieve the instructional goal. Evaluation instruments demonstrate that teachers can change their classroom behavior as a result of inservice training and can increase their self-sufficiency and confidence in working with problem learners.

Two models used in these courses are the school-based model and the clinical model:

- *The school-based model* involves training at the school where the teachers work. Generally, a large proportion of the staff at the school takes the course, lending mutual support and assistance for changes that occur as a result of training. One advantage of this model is that teachers can easily be provided with supervision of their classroom teaching skills by course instructors. A variation of this model is the multi-school-based model, where inservice training is rotated among a few participating schools.
- *The clinical model* involves training through supervised teaching experiences in a clinical setting. Unfortunately, inservice participants usually come from different schools, with no single school fully represented, thus reducing support among colleagues at each teacher's school. Also, teachers are not working with their own students. This may result in a lessened ability to carry over new instructional strategies to the home school. However, this model has the advantage of potentially closer supervision of the teachers throughout the course.

In addition to the use of these two models in the courses described, there are two different techniques for teaching the "What Works" method. In one course, the dialogue is introduced by first having the teachers themselves experience the process through group interaction and role play, then by having them apply the method in their own classrooms. In a few instances, two teachers teamed their effort to solve the instructional problems of a student they had in common. In the second course, teachers were taught the "What Works" method first through a case study example, then by observing the method used in a team meeting among teachers, and finally by participating themselves in a team planning meeting at their own schools.

AN INSERVICE COURSE USING A SCHOOL-BASED MODEL

This inservice course took place in a public elementary school located in a middle-income area with some students bussed from nearby lower-income neighborhoods. The training site was a small, traditional self-contained school with a special education wing for students with early childhood problems and/or orthopedic handicaps. The group of teachers that took part in this inservice training was composed of six regular and seven special education teachers, as well as two administrators, all participating on a voluntary basis. These people represented about half of both the regular and special teacher population at the school. University or recertification credits were available for those participating in the course.

Course Content

Fifteen two-hour sessions held at the school included topics in the following areas:

- Identification, clarification, and communication of classroom instructional problems using the "What Works" method.
- Instructional methods and strategies for problem students in regular classrooms in the areas of reading, mathematics, and behavior management.
- Task analysis and its relationship to instructional planning.

In addition to weekly class assignments, each participant chose a project related to the classroom application of course material. This involved the identification and analysis of a particular problem, the use of selected strategies to solve the problem, and the evaluation of the method's success.

The course began with an introduction to the "What Works" method. The planning system's five steps were explained through description and examples. Teachers were then asked to participate in the problem-solving dialogue by discussing their concerns about how the programs in their schools work with handicapped learners. Many concerns were voiced, including the following:

- Too much time elapses between student referral and testing.
- Children do not have anything to work on when they return to the regular classroom.
- There is inadequate planning between teacher and specialist.
- The student's regular teacher has no training in special education.
- Behavior management programs are inconsistent when a child

moves to the resource setting.

- Problem children have poor attendance records, causing them to miss work.
- Individualized work for one child in a class of 25 students is an overwhelming demand on the teacher's time and resources.

Teachers explored these concerns through discussion. They then focused on a pattern of concerns embedded in the above statements which related to the separate responsibilities of the regular and special teachers. While many regular teachers thought that the special teacher should assume a major responsibility for the instructional planning of the handicapped child, the special teachers believed the opposite. A lack of communication and a failure to solve problems jointly was evident in these statements.

Using this issue to demonstrate the "What Works" method, a special teacher and a regular teacher who had worked with a particular student were paired to plan jointly for that student's instructional program. They addressed each of the problem-solving steps, identifying the areas of concern, the child's positive accomplishments, strategies that had worked in the past with the child, and a plan for achieving particular goals. In the second class the teachers worked together again to determine what strategies had worked, what goals had been accomplished, and what the next plan would be. Any new or continued concerns became the subject for working through the process again in the ongoing evaluation of the student's progress. During this activity, teachers used forms printed with the five problem-solving steps to keep a record of their ideas and plans from one week to the next. This record acted as a source for instructional objectives and as a record of the student's progress. During the third class, dialogue occurred between a teacher, student, and parent. Monitored by an instructor experienced in the method, the conference centered on the concerns of the three parties with respect to the child's behavior. Each participant arrived at reachable goals, and they agreed upon strategies to assist the child in attaining their goals. By the end of the first three sessions, teachers could describe and demonstrate the "What Works" dialogue. They were beginning to identify more precisely their concerns about a particular student's performance in class. They were focusing on the positive accomplishments of their students and those strategies which had proven successful in the past. Furthermore, they were expressing more confidence in their ability to solve instruction problems in their own classrooms.

Training then focused upon the application of the "What Works" dialogue to instructional problems in the areas of math, reading, and the content areas. Adaptive techniques for addressing student learning differences were presented in each of the subject areas as well as behavior management. For example, one inservice session was devoted to a lecture and discussion about learning differences in math. Teachers were asked to select a child from their class, analyze how the student mastered a particular assignment, and develop an instructional strategy for further success based on that analysis. This exercise focused on the "What Works" question "What strategies work with this student?" in order to draw from the teacher her past success in related experiences.

A similar approach was taken during inservice sessions on reading. While several strategies were presented, such as providing context clues to help decode a word, or presentation of unfamiliar words within the context of word families, teachers were encouraged not only to use these strategies but to generate their own, as they determined what worked for them in specific problem situations.

In behavior management, many different approaches were presented, including the Glasser class meeting, management techniques such as consistent reinforcement, ignoring unproductive behaviors and rewarding productive ones, and contracting for achievement of specific behavioral goals. In applying these strategies, teachers were encouraged to state their concerns, to develop both attainable and measurable goals for the problem student, and to use strategies that were most closely related to the student's previous success.

These supervised classroom applications helped teachers to apply the content taught in inservice training. The use of the "What Works" dialogue, moreover, encouraged teachers to generate other strategies for solving instructional problems. Thus, each instructor drew from her past successes in the area of a particular concern to devise the most effective approach to the student's problem. The resulting plan of action reflected the teacher's individualized application of inservice content to her own specific classroom conditions.

As a final course project, several teachers chose to work together. One team effort between teachers, described next, led to a more successful instructional program for one student and a change in attitude on the part of his teachers.

Using "What Works" to Help David

David, a primary-level child in the orthopedic wing of the school, was experiencing problems in both his classroom and his physical therapy sessions. He cried readily for unknown reasons and would not indicate why he was in distress. Although capable, he would not respond to questions that demanded only simple "yes" or "no" answers. His teachers became convinced that their own frustrations would prevent the change of this unproductive behavior.

Using "What Works," the teachers analyzed the problem situation in their own classes. Following are the questions and responses used by David's physical therapist and academic teacher to resolve their concerns. (The authors wish to acknowledge Clareen Heikel and Ruth Flahive, who contributed this case study.)

What is the problem? In other words, what specifically is the behavior that is of most concern at this time?

- David cries frequently during physical therapy.
- David usually does not give answers to direct questions about his crying.
- David does not communicate why he is in distress.

- David demonstrates very little spontaneous speech.

After stating as many concerns as they could think of, David's teachers reviewed their list and identified two related areas of concern: David's frequent crying and his tendency not to talk. It appeared that David tended to rely upon crying more than speech as a coping mechanism. His teachers wanted to reduce the crying behavior and increase his verbal communication. With this selected concern in mind, his teachers addressed the next question.

What are the child's positive accomplishments? In other words, what does the child do well? What are some positive statements that can be made about him?

- Once David did not cry for the first twenty minutes of a physical therapy session.
- Once he brought a toy to therapy and answered questions about it.
- He then answered "yes" and "no" to other questions asked of him during that session.
- When prompted in his academic class, David answered questions directed to him about one-sixth of the time.
- He said, "I'm finished," once after completing a puzzle.

The list above reflects a number of David's positive accomplishments in relation to the concerns of reducing his crying and increasing his oral communication. His teachers referred back to this list as they answered the third "What Works" question.

What strategies work with the child? In other words, what have you tried with David that has shown positive results? Under what conditions has he been successful with respect to the problem behavior?

- He did not cry as much when it was explained in advance what was going to happen in therapy.
- He talked more frequently and reduced his crying when he brought a toy to therapy and when the toy was incorporated into activities that met therapeutic objectives.
- Crying decreased when more time was spent talking to him.
- When David began to cry, therapy stopped and the teacher explained what she was doing. She also put a time limit on the activity, explaining, "We'll do this until I count to 100."
- His teacher explained to him in advance that he was expected to tell her when he finished his work.

By now David's teachers began to realize that he, in fact, had experienced some positive accomplishments in their classes. Furthermore, there were strategies they had used in the past which proved successful in relation to the current area of concern. With increased awareness of what bothered them about David and what worked to improve his behavior in this area, his teachers addressed the other "What Works" questions.

What are the goals for the child? In other words, what are reasonable short-term goals for resolving the problem, based on what is known of the child's achievements and abilities?

- David's crying can decrease to the degree that it does not interfere with his physical therapy.

- David can express his needs and feelings verbally, using such short phrases as "Hi," "I'm finished," "my bus," and "help."

What are the plans for achieving the goals? In other words, based on what is known about the child's positive attributes and about strategies that are successful, how will the goals be accomplished? Following is the plan developed by David's physical therapist:

- David was encouraged to bring a game or a toy to each therapy session. It became a part of regular therapeutic activities.
- More emphasis was placed at first on relating and talking to David, with reduced physical therapy requirements. He was told what to expect throughout the session. As his crying decreased and his talking increased, the physical requirements were increased.
- Questions were phrased in such a way as to require a single word or phrase response. Prompting was given if David did not answer. Responses were rewarded.

David's academic teacher used different strategies in her plan but worked toward the same goals:

- She explained to David each day what was expected of him.
- She rewarded David with a picture sticker every time he spoke to her or the therapist ("yes" or "no" responses did not count).
- She used a time-out strategy for five minutes if David did not respond to required answers or multiple-choice answers within 30 seconds.

Even though David's teachers had coordinated a plan to work with him, they both continued to be concerned about their negative attitudes toward him. They felt these attitudes had contributed to a vicious cycle which interfered with David's progress, and they were fearful that the cycle might continue in spite of their new plan. Thus, in addition to developing a plan for David, each teacher addressed the first three "What Works" questions in relation to her own feelings. Following are the written responses of the physical therapist to these questions:

What are my concerns?

- I want to maintain my concentration on achieving specific therapeutic activities (e.g., back extension, hip and knee extension, equilibrium reactions) despite David's crying.
- I am frustrated and angry because David cries or is silent when I try to find the reason for his distress.
- I have not attempted to seek David out for conversation or play as I do other children.

The physical therapist felt that the frustration and anger she felt when David cried was her area of greatest concern. She addressed the next two "What Works" questions with this concern in mind.

What are my positive accomplishments in reducing my frustration as I work with David?

- I have made special efforts to talk with David in a non-therapeutic situation (e.g., during play time in the classroom).

- I have been able to anticipate a successful activity for him to do. I have asked him to do it and allowed him time to complete the task independently.
- In therapy situations, I have tried to talk to him about farm animals and farm activities (he lives on a farm) as well as activities that he is doing in the classroom, letting therapy objectives take a secondary role.

What worked? How was I able to do these positive things?

- I admitted to myself that getting angry with him and a "you have to do this" attitude did not work and actually increased his distress.
- I gave David the benefit of the doubt that he cannot formulate words or produce vocalizations when he is under stress, and I was able to anticipate when and what would make him cry. I began to explain the sequence of what was going to happen and why. Also, since he cannot express himself or state reasons for his distress, I began to speak for him, "You are hurting or feeling badly. Is . . . the problem?" He could then answer with a "yes" or "no."
- I became more playful. I brought a toy or a game to therapy and used it to begin a therapy session or incorporated it into activities.

This physical therapist's analysis of her attitude toward David's behavior allowed her to become more aware of her feelings and how she might direct them positively. The exercise enhanced her understanding of the effects of her behavior on her student and provided her with insights that could be used to develop an effective plan of therapy. This demonstrates the success of the "What Works" method. When the teacher addressed her own feelings of frustration, she could then move on to implement successfully those strategies which addressed David's therapeutic needs.

David's teachers implemented their plans right away. The following is a record kept by David's academic teacher of the changes she observed.

> *Monday:* The plan was explained to David about what would happen when he did or did not respond verbally to questions asked in class. During table work he said, "I'm finished," after his first task was completed. He refused to respond after completing his second task. He was timed-out seven times until he responded with, "I'm finished." While timed-out he cried at first. However, he had eleven positive responses that day. Each was rewarded with a picture sticker. I was not angry or frustrated during this intervention. I had a definite plan and knew what I had to do.
>
> *Tuesday:* Again the plan was explained to David. He stated that he understood the plan. He had no time-outs and 16 positive responses. He seemed pleased with himself and his pictures.
>
> *Wednesday:* Same procedure. One time-out with six positive responses. The type of activities for the day did not require many verbal responses.
>
> *Thursday:* No time-outs and eight positive responses. He seems happy and not particularly concerned with getting the picture rewards.

His verbal responses, although prompted, were expressed naturally without stress or hesitation on his part.
Monday: Responded enthusiastically. No time-outs.

About her plan, David's physical therapist wrote:

I feel that there has been a considerable reduction in my feelings of despair as a result of (1) having defined a consistent method of handling David's crying behavior, and (2) having seen a change in David's behavior which has led to productive therapy sessions. David is readily responding verbally the majority of the time. This is now happening without the use of a concrete reward . . . I have gained more understanding of the difficulties David must experience . . . and more insight into how important it is to David that I let him know that I am aware of what he may be feeling, fearing, or wanting by verbalizing for him and getting his affirmative or negative response. The ability to express himself spontaneously must be a later step. Seeing David smile and being able to share his sense of humor has been very satisfying. Specific therapeutic objectives can now be worked towards without a struggle!

Within a month David had clearly met the objectives of the plan developed for him using the "What Works" dialogue. His teachers continued to monitor his progress on these objectives but met again to develop new plans for other areas of concern. This evaluating and planning cycle became an integral part of his instructional program.

A key point made through this example is that the child's teachers had within themselves the resources to solve what appeared to be an overwhelming instructional problem. The child's problem demanded an awareness of the child's behavior, its effect upon the teachers' own attitudes, and a knowledge of previously successful strategies. While information about behavioral principles and adaptive strategies was critical to the solution of the problem just described, it is evident that David's teachers also were able to draw upon their own experiences with him to develop a successful plan of instruction.

The Results of Inservice Training

By the end of this inservice program, teachers were able to solve a number of instructional problems in their classrooms. To determine their own perceptions about what they had learned, the regular teachers were asked the following questions at the end of training:

- How many children in your classroom leave the room at any time during the week for resource services?
- Of this number, how many of these children do you believe you could instruct appropriately without resource room placement, or with only resource teacher consultation?

Responses to these questions indicated that, of the 29 resource children reportedly in the classrooms of regular teachers who participated, 19 of these children, or 65 percent, were perceived by the teachers as not needing direct resource room services (while there had been an earlier referral). While there is no pre-course data to show a pattern of change relating to these questions, the numbers might be interpreted as an optimistic sign that regular teachers felt more confident in their ability to work with handicapped children in the classroom.

The evaluation of this course also addressed changes in the classroom behavior of teachers (Swanson 1980). The measurement instrument used was the Classroom Strategies Observation (CSO), a low inference device intended to determine whether there were observable changes in the number and variety of instructional strategies used by the regular teacher. It focused on two children each teacher had identified as having learning or behavior problems. Observers also simultaneously recorded the instructional strategies used with any child in the class regardless of learning characteristics or problems. Both types of data were then clarified by means of post-observation interviews with the teachers. It was expected that recorded strategies used with any child in the class would present a more accurate picture of the teacher's total repertoire of strategies, whereas recordings related to children who were difficult to work with would provide insight into a teacher's problem-solving proficiency and understanding of children with learning problems. Trained graduate students in education made four 30-minute observations of every regular teacher in the school before and after the inservice training, recording the number and variety of strategies the teacher used, a list of which was developed through field-testing.

Results using the CSO suggested that those teachers who participated in problem solving training ("What Works") demonstrated a significant total mean increase of 5.6 strategies per regular teacher working with any student in the class ($t = 4.63$, $df = 5$, $p < .05$). Those teachers also increased in their range of strategies (variety), while others who did not take the course showed little change in number or variety of their instructional methods. Looking at the students who were experiencing problems in class, the mean number of strategies used per teacher taking the course increased by 3.6 strategies (6.0 to 9.6). There were no apparent shifts among those teachers not taking the course.

The strategies used with problem learners most commonly observed among teachers who took the course were as follows:

- Breaking down a task until a child succeeded.
- Helping a student decode a word.
- Use of teaching aids to supplement instruction.
- Presenting a task in a variety of ways.
- Peer tutoring.

Many of the strategies used by teachers in the course to work with problem learners were also observed in the teachers' interactions with the class as a whole. This suggests that instructional strategies and problem solving skills taught to teachers to help their handicapped students can encourage alternative methods of instruction with students who are not handicapped.

AN INSERVICE COURSE USING THE CLINICAL MODEL

This inservice course enrolled ten regular and ten special education teachers and was held in conjunction with a special education summer institute. The institute operated a clinic serving 40 handicapped students. The regular and special education teachers who participated in this credited inservice came from both elementary and secondary schools in the district and met for formalized instruction during the first week of the course, then taught or observed for four weeks in the summer clinic. A one-day seminar each week allowed teachers to integrate their observations and teaching techniques with the material presented in the course. Two instructors, one from the local school system and one from the university, provided leadership for both seminars and the summer school.

Inservice instruction was directed at assisting teachers in accomplishing the following objectives:

- Knowledge of the legal responsibilities of the regular teacher towards the handicapped students in their classes
- Knowledge of the diagnostic-prescriptive process used to instruct and plan for special students in the regular classroom
- Awareness of a variety of conditions that cause learning problems
- Skill in applying instructional strategies in the classroom setting with problem learners
- Improved communication between regular and special teachers
- Application of the "What Works" method to teaching and evaluating problem learners in the regular classroom

This course differed from the one previously described not only because it followed a clinical model, but also because it applied the "What Works" method along with other sources of data about the child. The "What Works" method was not used as the primary means for responding to the needs of the student, but as one of the many sources of information, including test scores and other diagnostic findings.

"What Works" was introduced during the first week of inservice training as a vehicle for improving communication between regular and special teachers and as a means for using student feedback to develop and evaluate instructional plans for problem learners. Teachers analyzed their students' instructional needs and successes, helping them to apply systematically the skills they acquired in the course. The teachers first were exposed to a case study which illustrated the use of "What Works." Then a demonstration was given that focused on the program of a particular child in the summer school. With the course instructor as facilitator, the student's parents and teachers met to discuss the child's progress and to develop further plans for instruction. The five organizing questions of the "What Works" method were addressed.

Each of these questions was developed through the use of the three sub-steps: brainstorming, exploring, and selecting. Brainstorming encouraged the open and unbiased participation of the teachers and parents. Next, the responses were explored with the following step: "What prompted you to say . . . ? Tell me more about . . . ." This review allowed for the expansion of ideas presented during brainstorming. As the teachers and parents explored their thoughts, a clearer picture of the student's behavior and instructional needs emerged. Finally the teachers and parents were asked to select the major problem revealed by this process. Frequently, this process caused the group to synthesize their ideas about the student's educational needs.

Following is an example of plans developed by teachers and parents using "What Works."

"What Works" With a Learning Disabled Student

Alex was a 12-year-old sixth-grader who was working at least two years below grade level in most areas. Alex's regular teachers, two special education teachers, the directors of the inservice program, and Alex's mother gathered for a conference to address Alex's needs. Although testing revealed that Alex had a severe problem in auditory memory, the focus of the meeting was on specific concerns observed by each of the participants. They assessed his instruction using "What Works."

What are your concerns about Alex's current progress? The ideas of all the participants were listed in the brainstorming step of this question.

- Alex will be confronted with material that is too difficult for him in middle school. He is behind in all academic subjects.
- Alex won't ask questions when he doesn't understand.
- Alex's difficulties sometimes go unnoticed by the teacher because he is quiet and cooperative.
- Alex's attention span is short, especially when the work is difficult for him. This may cause problems for him in the open-setting classroom he is scheduled for in September.
- At times Alex works very slowly. He does not tell his teacher when he needs more time.

Later, in the selection step, these statements were analyzed into a pattern which served to summarize the various ideas. One pattern was Alex's reluctance to communicate his needs, particularly when he does not understand difficult material. This appeared to be a reasonable concern to address during the inservice course and one which all the participants agreed upon.

What can Alex do successfully?

- His work is often neat, organized, and completed, when he's given enough time to do so.
- He has a good attitude toward school work and a desire to learn.
- He plays soccer and baseball successfully and taught his sisters how to play tennis.
- He is very responsible and appears to be accepted by both peers and adults.
- He has a neat appearance.
- He is very enterprising (for example, he collected returnable cans to help pay for a vacation trip).

What made it possible for this student to succeed? The team discussed several factors that made Alex's successes possible; including, interested parents, his motivation to learn, his willingness to complete an assignment that was not too difficult for him, his pleasant disposition, and his good motor coordination in games.

What should Alex's goals be?

- To improve his academic performance
- To increase the rate at which Alex can complete assignments
- To increase his assertiveness, or willingness to communicate his needs, with the teacher

The group focused on Alex's assertiveness during the summer sessions of inservice training. This focus was consistent both with the goals set for Alex and with the teachers' feelings that success in these areas would lead to success in his academic subjects as well. The teachers also thought that these goals could be accomplished during the short period of time they were working with Alex in the inservice course.

What strategies will be used to achieve these goals? All members of the group agreed that they would encourage Alex to ask questions when he did not understand something either in class or at home. They would prompt him to request help whenever it appeared necessary.

The "What Works" dialogue was used to develop a strategy for assisting Alex. The goal was to help him to assume more responsibility for communicating his learning needs to his teachers. In addition, the diagnostic test results were used in formulating plans for him. These plans were based upon what teachers knew of Alex's academic needs, learning successes, and the results of testing.

The following school year, both Alex and his mother reported that he was experiencing more success in school. He was more proficient at communicating his needs to his teachers, and the resource teacher at his middle school was monitoring his program and continuing to help Alex grow in his assertiveness in school.

Course Evaluation

A self-report survey was distributed before and after the course to examine teachers' growth in knowledge of the teaching strategies presented. On a five-point Likert scale measuring the knowledge of class topics, there was a four-point shift in the area of teachers' self-perceptions of their knowledge of the "What Works" method ($p < .001$). This was the greatest shift on the scale with respect to all the strategies listed. Teachers also rated the strategies according to their assessment of their usefulness in the home and school settings. In these ratings "What Works" received an average of 4.38 points out of five possible points, the highest rating assigned by teachers to any of the 17 instructional strategies taught in the course.

One teacher spoke of the ability of the "What Works" method to maintain the attention of all group members during lengthy staff meetings. Teachers valued the intrinsic organization the process imposed and the plan for instruction that resulted. Many teachers reported that their responses were in direct contrast to their feelings about the conventional team meetings they had experienced in their own schools. Many also stated that this problem solving process actually enhanced their participation and communication in the multidisciplinary setting. Another evaluation focused on the free exchange of ideas with the parent. Some teachers were amazed at the wealth of information contributed by parents both in examples of success and in suggested strategies for instruction. Furthermore, teachers were pleased that they were able to identify areas in which they had worked appropriately with the student and had contributed to that student's success. They had expressed confidence in the educational plans that they had developed using "What Works."

SUMMARY

This chapter described two different inservice uses of the "What Works" method. One approach involved a school based model with "What Works" as the primary framework for developing a student's instructional plan. The other approach involved a clinical model which used "What Works" as one of many potential strategies that may lead to a student's instructional plan. In both settings the dialogue proved successful in helping teachers to draw upon their own knowledge about successful strategies with particular problem students. The result was both a plan which was more appropriate to the needs of individual students and a feeling of increased confidence among teachers in their ability to work with a variety of learners in their classrooms.

REFERENCES

Essexville-Hampton Public Schools. 1975. *Project FAST: adopter/facilitator information.* Essexville-Hampton Public Schools. (ERIC Document Reproduction Service No. ED 117 925)

Ringlaben, R. P., and Price, J. R. 1981. Regular classroom teachers' perceptions of mainstreaming effects. *Exceptional Children* 47:302-304.

Swanson, E. F. 1980. A study of an inservice training program to help teachers work with special needs children in the regular classroom. *Dissertation Abstracts International* 40(11-A):5830.

U. S. Department of Education. 1984. *Sixth annual report to Congress on the implementation of Public Law 94-142: The Education for All Handicapped Children Act.* Washington, D. C.: U. S. Department of Education.

"What Works" in College Counseling

Ruth Talbott Kemig, EdD

Until recently, failure has been accepted as a normal condition of college life. A 1972 study showed that the nation's academic institutions, including the most selective, eliminated half of their students before graduation (Roueche and Snow 1977, p. 7). Another study, published in 1970, estimated that more than 380,000 students yearly experienced the trauma and dislocation of academic dismissal (Maxwell 1979, p. 7). Among underprepared students in the 1970s, the attrition was even higher; 90 percent failed to complete successfully the compensatory programs which they undertook, a dismal record considering the resources which were expended on these programs (Roueche and Snow 1977, p. 8).

The current resurgence of interest in salvaging college students is a result as much of demographic changes as of humanitarian concerns. The dwindling supply of young people to replace presently enrolled students has caused the prevention of failure to become a survival issue for colleges and has spawned a host of practices designed to prevent failure and thereby to reduce attrition. Colleges have expanded support services and compensatory courses, changed their requirements, inflated student grades, established improved orientation and advising, and made many other accommodations to students.

Yet failure persists. Despite the efforts of many faculty and administrators, too many students avoid genuine involvement in their courses, ignore the early warning signs of academic difficulty, underutilize support services, and bypass their advisors, apparently indifferent to their marginal (or worse) achievement.

There is evidence to suggest that contemporary students' failure to learn is attributable, at least in part, to student characteristics other than the fact of their lacking a particular skill or body of information. Learning problems in college are best understood when they are considered in the context of a student's previous experiences in schools. Today's students have been acculturated in society at large and in their high schools in particular to a cluster of behaviors which inhibit learning and are disastrous in college (Levine 1980).

Large numbers of students on college campuses are victims of learned helplessness. Helplessness affects the bright student who coasted through high school and is overwhelmed by early failures in the more demanding college environment, as well as affecting the chronically poor student whose efforts have been repeatedly met with inexplicable rewards (passing grades) or recurring punishment (failing grades). According to Roueche (1981), helplessness victims *lack motivation, do not seem willing to try, are not able to associate results with effort, are often defensive and will not respond assertively.* "Since the behavior associated with learned helplessness seems deadly to the learning experience, it is important to discover an approach, an attitude that will counter the phenomenon" (Roueche, pp. 36-37).

How can students be helped to assume responsibility for their learning in college? This is the central issue, the critical task for planners, instructors, and counselors–to utilize the experiences and contents of instruction in such a way that students become responsible for their own learning.

THE "WHAT WORKS" METHOD

"What Works" is a method of working with students so that they become responsible for their own learning. It is a method of capitalizing on a critical moment when a student is concerned about an academic problem and therefore is most receptive to participating with an academic counselor in a helpful learning experience. It is also a method for the student to develop problem solving skills, by applying the "What Works" steps to the troublesome academic situation and by modeling the counselor's techniques. Each academic accomplishment becomes the basis for generalizing the learning strategies which have worked to other academic needs. The student participating in "What Works," therefore, accomplishes not only the specific learning task which is required for a course, but also develops awareness of how he/she has learned and can learn in other similar situations. The student acquires both a set of steps to solve other study problems and the knowledge about how to study effectively.

The "What Works" method is an open-ended question and answer procedure which helps students think through their academic problems and take actions to solve them. Counselors ask questions rather than tell students what to do. Counselors ask questions about "islands of competency" within the area of concern–that is, about the things which the student has done well. Counselors focus on successes in the problem area and ask what made those successes possible, rather than diagnose the failure of learning which caused the student to be assigned or referred. The counselor looks to future success, and seeks out the student's own skills and methods which, when applied to the problem area, will bring about success there as well.

"What Works" has three specific goals for the student.

1. *Awareness.* The student becomes aware of how he learns, of his own goals, and of the options he has for improving the situation he is in. He focuses on those particulars in himself and his situation which are resources for solving this problem.
2. *Plan.* The student makes a plan which includes a goal statement, the steps which he will do to achieve the goal, and a time to review his accomplishment to see if the goal has been achieved and to reflect on how he achieved it.
3. *Responsibility for "What Works."* The student learns the steps of the "What Works" method of solving problems and utilizes this method of thinking things through, making a plan and carrying it out in other challenging situations.

The counselor asks questions to clarify the problem and to guide the student to an awareness of the student's own resources for solving it. The five basic questions, an optional sixth question, and the order they are most effectively used are as follows.

1. What is the problem?
2. What has gone well for you?
3. What worked? How?
4. What do you want to see happen?
5. How can you make it happen? Make a plan.
6. You have done really well on ____ and ____. What is working for you now?

The academic counseling situation also provides resources which the counselor draws from in order to help the student.

1. *The Particular Content To Be Learned.* The content to be learned by the student includes the course content as well as the appropriate techniques for effective study and the responsible student actions. In "What Works," the acquisition of academic material is both an end in itself and the means to the larger purpose of providing a first-hand experience in effective learning and problem solving.
2. *A Critical Moment.* The student, having sought assistance, has a recognized problem and a need to learn. The events which cause students to seek help—perhaps receiving a difficult assignment or a failing grade—have heightened their awareness and helped to create a moment when they are receptive to learning new strategies. These elements of immediacy and relevance to personally important goals are considered by developmental theorists to be essential for learning progress (Roueche and Snow 1977, p. 13), yet are impossible to achieve in the isolated settings in which learning skills are traditionally taught (Keimig 1983).
3. *Goals and Methodology.* The counselor provides goals and a way for the student to learn from experience. True competence is

achieved, not through memorization, but through analytical problem solving activities (Chickering 1969, pp. 324-5; Whimbey and Lockhead 1981). In "What Works," the student's knowledge about how to study is developed experientially, through the processes of analyzing and applying previously successful practices, rather than through lectures or other passive (for the student) methods.

4. *Counselor Contact Time.* The academic counselor has time to work patiently with a student, to "connect significantly with those concerns of central importance" to the student (Chickering 1969, p. 3). Students respond positively to a personalized academic environment.
5. *Counselor Interaction.* The counselor's responses are potent resources for reinforcing, clarifying, teaching, and affirming values. A student counselor's attention and friendship can also provide peer modeling and emotional support to students who have a difficult time finding acceptance in the college community.

GETTING STARTED WITH "WHAT WORKS"

Solving a problem involves several more or less sequential thinking processes. The "What Works" basic questions and their many variations are the tool which the counselor uses to get the student thinking in effective ways for problem solving. Understanding the thinking processes which are necessary for problem solving helps the counselor to recognize when to persist with questions directed at one thought process, and when to move on to the next. The first two of these processes—exploring and specifying—are the keys to achieving greater awareness and to designing relevant plans that work.

Process 1. Exploration. For each basic question, exploration is necessary, so that all the relevant possibilities are considered. As students become more aware in response to the counselor's questions, they will notice aspects of the situation which were not in their thinking when the conference began. Often these later answers are the ones people select as the most important, so the counselor rarely accepts the first answer to a question as sufficient. Other possibilities are sought through further questioning and brainstorming.

Process 2. Specification. Specification refers to thinking about identifiable parts ("I set the problem up correctly but I had the wrong answers") instead of generalities ("I bombed out on the math test yesterday"). Thinking in specifics puts boundaries on what is not known and allows specific successes to be recognized; thinking about specifics also leads to identifiable steps which can be taken to achieve success. Problems cannot be solved and are very discouraging to the person whose thinking is stuck in generalities.

Often the counselor's questions are alternately the exploring type (to stimulate thinking of more ideas) and the specifying type (to achieve better understanding of the particular situation and the student's specific learning needs). To explore further, the counselor modifies "What is the problem" by asking "What else bothers you in . . ."; to get more specific information, the counselor rephrases and asks, "I am not clear on . . ." or "Describe the class and tell me what is happening when . . ." The counselor continues the exploring and specifying processes, by asking the first question in many different ways until the student has provided several ideas about the specific difficulties being experienced in the course. Figure 5.1. shows some alternate ways of asking "What is the problem" to achieve the exploration and specification processes.

In a similar way, the "What Works" second question "What has gone well for you" is alternately explored and specified when the counselor asks, "When have you been successful with . . ." or "What went well on the tests in . . ." (See Figure 5.2.).

"What worked . . . How" is explored and specified until many ideas have been elicited by the counselor asking, "How did you study" or "How did you do this one" (See Figure 5.3.).

"What do you want to see happen" is the question which will lead to a plan. However, vague student responses such as "I want to do better in . . ." are not helpful. Of course they want to do better! The counselor asks, "What would you like to see happen" or "What would you like to have happen by next week." In so doing, the counselor focuses the student's attention on specific goals which, when achieved, will contribute to the larger more general goal of doing better in the course.

Process 3. Selection. For each basic question, when all of the relevant factors seem to have been discussed, the student selects that which is most important. From the student's responses to the counselor's queries about the problem, the student selects that which is more pressing or difficult now. From the several responses to the counselor's repeated queries about what has gone well in the problem area, the student selects that which is more important to him/her. From the student's responses to the counselor's continued queries about what worked to make that previous success possible, the student chooses that action which contributed the most.

Selection gives control to the student at each stage of problem solving. Selection also encourages the student to believe that there are options, and that the student can choose to do things which will lead to success.

Process 4. Synthesis. Synthesis refers to putting ideas together from several sources. The student's plan is a synthesis primarily of the ideas expressed in response to earlier questions, particularly to the questions about what has worked. The plan may also include a counselor suggestion or ideas obtained from how-to-study materials, other students, or the course instructor.

Process 5. Generalization. Students generalize when they recognize similar learning situations in which a previously successful study approach will work. The more situations in which an idea can be seen to work, the more the student will feel able to use it again.

Figures 5.1.-5.6. contain many versions of the "What Works" basic questions. Beside the questions on the left is the goal to be achieved through the use of the question (awareness, a plan, or responsibility for the "What Works" method). On the right side of each figure is the thought process which the counselor seeks to develop (exploration, specification, selection, synthesis, summarization, generalization) through the use of the various forms of the questions.

"WHAT WORKS" IN ACTION

The dialogues which follow have been collected from the records and observations of three years' collective experience with the "What Works" method, in a learning assistance center in a medium-size four-year college. Within the learning center, all staff, including instructors, graduate assistants, and student counselors became proficient with the "What Works" method and used it consistently with their counselees. In each of the cases which follow, the counselor has modified the basic questions and has used the full planning process only when it was needed.

The Initial Conference

During the first conference, the student's reasons for seeking assistance determines what follows. Students who come to the center because their instructors have assigned particular tasks to be accomplished may be well aware of their learning needs and may therefore require little further assistance; or students may deny their needs and act defensively or angrily. Other students seeking assistance because they are doing poorly usually have very inadequate knowledge of the specific kinds of study activities which they must do in order to learn. Their discouragement is compounded when they sincerely perceive themselves to be working and trying very hard, as when they have naively resolved to "do better on the midterm exam" and then failed that as well.

The use of the "What Works" dialogue, its first question focused on defining the problem, provides the counselor with the information necessary to ascertain how effectively the student is operating to solve the immediate study problem. The counselor adjusts the "What Works" process accordingly. When a counselee's responses show a high degree of awareness and that appropriate study steps are being undertaken, the counselor shortens the "What Works" process. Offering positive feedback ("That is really a good way to learn . . .") or a suggestion ("Did you notice the practice exercises at the end of the chapter?"), the counselor affirms the value of what the student has done and encourages his/her self-reliant efforts.

When students' responses are negative ("I'm sick and tired of this Mickey Mouse stuff" or "I hate math–I never could do it" or "This assignment is stupid") or unrealistic ("I failed the first test, but I just have to get an *A* at midterm and then I'll be all right . . ."), the counselor works through

FIGURE 5.1. *Achieving Awareness with "What Is The Problem?"*

Achieving Awareness with "WHAT IS THE PROBLEM?"

Questions	*Process*
"What are your concerns about ____________?"	EXPLORATION
"How are things going in ____________?"	
"What else concerns you?"	
"Brainstorm a list."	
"What is bugging you in ____________?"	
"I'm not clear on ____________."	SPECIFICATION
"It would help me to know ____________."	
"What worries you the most?"	SELECTION
"Which is most urgent?"	

FIGURE 5.2. *Achieving Awareness with "What Has Gone Well For You?"*

Achieving Awareness with "WHAT HAS GONE WELL FOR YOU?"

Questions	*Process*
"What has gone well for you with ____________ ?"	EXPLORATION
"When were you successful with ____________ ?"	
"When did you ____________ ?"	
"I would like to know more about ____________ ."	SPECIFICATION
"What went well on this test?"	
"Show me ____________ ."	
"Which achievement do you feel best about?"	SELECTION
"Which achievement meant most to you?"	

FIGURE 5.3. *Achieving Awareness of Options with "What Worked? How?"*

Achieving Awareness of Options with "WHAT WORKED? HOW?"

Questions	*Process*
"When did you take this test?"	EXPLORATION
"Is that what worked, doing/being ________ ?"	
"How did you study?"	
"What else worked?"	
"How did you do this one?"	SPECIFICATION
"You said you reviewed ________ . What did you do to review?"	
"Get back into the scene. What helped you?"	
"You liked ________ . What made it happen?"	
"What do you think is the most important thing you did?"	SELECTION
"What is the clearest statement of what worked?"	

FIGURE 5.4. *Planning with "What Do You Want To See Happen?"*

Planning with "WHAT DO YOU WANT TO SEE HAPPEN?"

Questions	*Process*
"What are your goals?"	EXPLORATION
"What would you like to see happen?"	
"You did __________. Is this still important to you?"	
"What do you want to see happen by the end of next week?"	SPECIFICATION
"You didn't like __________. What would the opposite be?"	
"What is the most important thing you want to see happen?"	SELECTION

FIGURE 5.5 *Planning with "How Can You Make It Happen? Make A Plan."*

Planning with "HOW CAN YOU MAKE IT HAPPEN? MAKE A PLAN."

Questions	*Process*
"Put together the most useful ideas. Make a plan."	SYNTHESIS
"Specify– *What (goal)* *How* *When* *What is the next step* *What should be done by our next meeting"*	SPECIFICATION
"Set a date."	
"Write out your goal statement and the steps in your plan."	
"When you return for your posttest (or review) conference, how will you know that you have been successful?"	

FIGURE 5.6. *Achieving Responsibility with "What Is Working For You Now?"*

Achieving Responsibility with "WHAT IS WORKING FOR YOU NOW?"

Questions	*Process*
"You have done well on ____________ . What is working for you now?"	SUMMARIZE
"This ____________ is really well done. How did you get it together?"	
"When are these things useful for you to do?"	GENERALIZE
"What is your most pressing study demand this week?"	
"What questions should you ask yourself to solve this study problem?"	

the entire dialogue. The counselor may not get far in the dialogue during the first conference, as in this situation.

Dialogue	Analysis
S. My anatomy instructor said I should come here. I got a *D* and an *F* on my first two tests and I really studied. I have a test next Tuesday and if I don't pass this one I will not get into nursing in the fall.	
C. Do you have time now to stay and talk about it? I believe I can help you.	
S. Yeah—I have 20 minutes before class.	
C. What is the problem with these tests?	
S. I just can't pass them. I really tried. *(S. is close to tears.)* I wouldn't feel so bad if I hadn't studied. But I went over everything.	C. Explores using "What Works." S. at this time has only general ideas and cannot solve her problem with these tests until she has a more precise understanding of what is causing her difficulty.
C. What are the anatomy tests like?	
S. They are short answer tests and they cover everything in the unit. Next week's test is on the heart and circulatory system.	
C. What seems difficult about these tests?	
S. I really don't know. *(More tears.)* I think I will do well, and then I get so many wrong	

C. Tests can really get you down! I'm sure I can help you . . . but we don't have time to really get into this now. Can you come back at three? Bring all of your study materials for anatomy—syllabus, tests, textbook, notes, Lab book. *(Putting her arm around S.)* Don't let it get you down! We'll work this out . . . .

C. Recognizes the need to do considerable exploring and specifying the problem, when S. is less upset.

At three o'clock—

C. I'm glad to see you again. I see you brought your anatomy things.

S. Yes—but Dr. . . . keeps the tests, so I don't have them.

C. I don't have a good understanding yet of why your studying is not paying off for you.

C. Rephrases "What is the problem?" to get the "What Works" dialogue going again.

C. *(Getting out a Problem Solving Guide.)* You have had a lot of experience as a successful student which can be a resource to you. The College has other resources too, to help with a study problem. I am going to ask you some questions to help us both understand the problem with these tests and determine your resources. Then we'll make notes and give you a copy so you will remember your plan. OK?

C. Explains the "What Works" program and the use of the Problem Solving Guide. *(The guide and techniques for introducing it are fully described in the next section.)*

C. Thinking back to the last test—What was the hardest part?

C. Begins "What Works" again, alternately exploring and asking specific questions.

S. Well, it covered these three chapters and the test questions came from all over. I think I did OK on the parts we'd gone over in Lab. The questions are so hard, you cannot be sure which answer is right because they seem so much alike.

C. You have some good ideas about what is making these tests hard—the parts you haven't gone over in Lab are more difficult and the questions with choices that seem so alike. What else made the test hard?

C. Provides praise for S. contribution, summarizes her ideas, and queries for more specific difficulties.

S. It all seems so familiar when I'm looking over my notes. But when I read the questions it's like I never saw that before.

C. What about your first test—what made that hard?

S. Well, I totally bombed that one. I didn't even recognize some of the words and we had to draw diagrams.

C. You have mentioned important things that are a problem for a lot of students—let me see if I have them all: not reviewing in class, choices when an-

C. Summarizes ideas of S., then asks S. to select the difficulty which will then be the focus of the rest of the "What Works" dialogue.

swers are so much alike, not recognizing words on the test, and having to draw diagrams. Which thing is *the most* difficult?

S. I would say that not reviewing in class and not remembering the right things. Some of those questions are like I never saw it before.

C. Have you ever studied science before?

C. Is shifting to "What has gone well for you?"

S. In high school, I took biology and chemistry.

C. How were those tests?

S. Much easier, I got *B* in biology and *C* in chemistry.

C. Which course do you feel best about?

C. Asks student to select the achievement which meant most to her.

S. Well, the biology because of the *B*. Also, it was a hard course and a lot of kids got *D*'s.

C. What did you do that helped you do so well on those biology tests?

C. Asks "What worked? How?"

S. Well, just what I'm doing now. I reviewed my notes and the answers to the questions we'd done for homework . . .

C. Questions, for homework? What questions?

C. Asks a specific question about a new idea.

S. Yes. Each week we had a set of homework questions to answer which we had to turn in. And the teacher gave them back to us to study for the test.

C. You have mentioned two really good techniques that you used to be so successful in biology. Can you think of anything else you did that helped?

C. Summarizes the ideas which helped, and queries for more ideas.

S. Well, the teacher went over everything the day before the test. They don't do that here. But that made such a difference.

C. It really does make a difference to have that organized review led by a teacher, but you're right —college instructors usually don't do it. Of all the things you have named, which do you think helped most?

C. Affirms the value of the review, and gives information through feedback about the responsibilities expected of instructors and students in college.

S. I think, uh, the homework questions and going over it in class. Those two things really.

C. The techniques you've mentioned are not only important for us to learn —but really necessary. We have to make choices about what to remember, because we can't remember everything in a chapter. The questions which your teacher gave you helped you know what was important. So did her review the day before the test.

C. Summarizes the important techniques that worked, and provides the information through feedback that these are necessary steps to learning.

C. What would you like to have happen?

C. Begins the planning phase by having S. formulate her goal.

S. I would like to have questions—that's impossible, I know, but I need to know what I should learn. Obviously I'm studying the wrong things.

C. Think back over your class time, and also over your study materials. What signals, aids, clues do you have that tell you what is important?

The rest of the dialogue with this student concerned techniques for directing her own study effort so that she spent her time on what was important to remember, and techniques for determining the importance of information. Her plan included (1) use her text's learning objectives and study aids (which had not been mentioned in class at all), (2) ask the instructor to clarify which objectives are most important, (3) turn the objectives into into questions and write the answers to them as her review method for tests, (4) make an appointment with the instructor to go over her tests and communicate her seriousness of purpose to the instructor, (5) return to see the counselor the day before the test to show her the questions and answers she's prepared, at which time the counselor will ask her some practice test questions, (6) return to the learning center after the course test, at which time the counselor and student will review the results.

The Follow-up Conference

The follow-up conference serves three important purposes: (1) the students demonstrate to the counselor (and themselves) that they have learned the content or overcome the difficulty for which they sought assistance, (2) students review the effectiveness of the specific actions they took to learn this material, and (3) students consider how to apply these effective methods to other areas in which they might be useful. The counselor uses this critical moment to provide feedback to the student and to affirm the value of the methods that the student has used and the achievement the student has demonstrated. The counselor uses one or two of the basic questions and frequent feedback to provide information and praise, to assess the effectiveness of this student's study effort, and to determine whether further assistance is needed.

The following is a presentation of a counselor's comments, directed toward a student who has taken an assigned posttest in nursing mathematics. The nursing instructor had assigned the review units following a mathematics test in class. (In this case, the first contact between the counselor and the student probably occurred in the conference when the posttest was being administered.)

Counselor's Comments	Analysis
C. You did really well–What did you do to prepare for this test?	C. Queries, alternately ex- exploring and asking for greater specification, to assure that the success (overall or success on individual items) is recognized and is savored a bit.
C. That was great–you have had so much trouble with this kind of question before.	C. Praises a specific achievement.
C. What worked? How did you do this one? What did you do to learn this material?	C. Queries, alternately exploring until specific steps have been identified.
C. *(Naming the study steps S. has used)* These are really effective. What other course assignments do you have coming up in the next few weeks where they would be useful?	C. Summarizes, then asks questions which lead students to generalize this new technique to other study areas.
C. *(Following a passed test)* What is the next topic which you have to review? What problem have you had with . . . ? *(Naming the topic)*	C. Begins "What Works" process anew, focusing on the new topic.
C. What is the problem here with this one?	C. Uses "What Works," briefly focusing on a missed question.
C. What worked for the others that you could use to learn the material (or to do this type of problem)?	

C. Do this one over again and try to do . . . *(Stating what worked before).* Or do this one over again and try . . . *(Offering a new suggestion).*	C. Reinforces an effective technique by providing on-site practice and praise, or suggests new ideas.
C. What would you like to have happen? How can you make it happen?	C. Encourages the further use of the more effective techniques even though a written plan is not prepared.

Writing A Plan

The Problem Solving Guide in Figure 5.7. and Figure 5.8. is a sample of a guide which is used to prepare written study plans. There are many advantages to writing out the steps of a plan, at least for some students. Students tend to forget the specifics of an unwritten plan. Furthermore, it is difficult to change old ways. Students may sincerely intend to carry out their study steps yet, when away from the counselor's positive influence, may drift back into their old habits. A written plan helps the student to persist with the new techniques. A written plan is clear and accurate, and focuses students' attention on their goals and on their specific responsibilities for learning the material.

Using the Problem Solving Guide also assists counselors and students to work with the basic questions and processes of the "What Works" method, and has these advantages:

1. Counselors and students quickly learn the questions and the systematic problem solving process.
2. A written plan is more likely to be followed.
3. Students learn the "What Works" process with a counselor, and then can take blank copies of the guide to use in their own problem solving.
4. The counselor who retains a carbon copy of the plan better remembers the specifics of the student's situation, and can respond more effectively.

As a practical point, not all students are introduced to the use of the Problem Solving Guide in the same way. The cooperative student, who is actively seeking to overcome a specific difficulty, is introduced to the guide early in the planning conference. Then the counselor begins the "What Works" dialogue and makes notes on the guide as the dialogue proceeds. For each question, the counselor highlights the ideas which the student selects as the most important. On the other hand, the resistant or difficult student is queried without introduction to the guide. The counselor uses the guide and makes notes, offering an explanation if and when the student asks. At the planning stage (after the five basic questions have been discussed), the coun-

FIGURE 5.7. *Problem Solving Guide (Side One).*

PROBLEM SOLVING GUIDE

1. *What is the problem?* (Be very specific. List at least three. Underline the most important one, then answer the rest of the questions about that one.)

2. *What have you done successfully in the area of your greatest concern?* (Describe several situations in which you have been successful with this problem. Underline the one that meant most to you.)

3. *How did you do this? What things worked?* (List specific things, as many as you can remember. Underline the one that was most important.)

4. *What would you like to see happen?*

5. *How can you make it happen?* (Use the other side to make a plan.)

FIGURE 5.8. ***Problem Solving Guide (Side Two).***

PLAN

GOAL: What? How much? How well? How long?

STEPS: How? Who? Where? When?

HOW WILL YOU KNOW WHEN YOU ARE SUCCESSFUL?

WHAT IS YOUR NEXT STEP?

selor suggests to the difficult student that they construct a plan. The counselor again asks the fourth "What Works" question and shares notes with the student. The student states a specific goal, which the counselor records.

GOALS OF USING "WHAT WORKS" IN ACADEMIC COUNSELING

Teaching Students Academic Skills

Academic counseling, whether done by instructors, specialists, counselors, or paraprofessionals, must provide information to students on how to study. How can the teaching of study skills be accomplished through the "What Works" dialogue? A major task of preparation for academic counseling is to become so thoroughly familiar with the basic methods of study that the person can respond appropriately with positive feedback and suggestions throughout the "What Works" dialogue. Course instructors must know the specific techniques which students need for their particular discipline and incorporate these into their teaching and conferences with students.

How much easier it would be to deliver a lecture on how to study! The students could make their own connections and adjust the study techniques described to their own problems. Unfortunately, lectures produce little change in behavior. The students who need academic assistance the most are those least adept at abstracting useful information from lectures. Furthermore, the lecturer's suggestions are often inappropriate, inasmuch as they do not take into account the individual study problems in a specific course and the learning styles of individual students.

On the other hand, the academic counselor uses three kinds of responses within the "What Works" method to teach and to make the connection between the student's experience and the study theory; (1) through *postive feedback* the counselor helps the student be aware of the effective techniques already in use, (2) through *suggestions* the counselor introduces alternative methods or adaptations to fit a particular need, (3) through *generalization* the counselor increases the student's knowledge about study skills and problem solving, and guides the student to an understanding of why these new skills and abilities have worked and how they can be utilized in other situations.

Academic skills, also called study skills, include those techniques that enhance understanding, improve recall, promote the ability to use information analytically, and enable students to prepare adequate papers, reports, and tests. These techniques are described fully in many fine texts which have been designed for student use. The important academic skills which students must utilize in college are:

1. Organize their study materials and environment
2. Schedule and plan their study time
3. Specify in detail their instructors' expectations and assignments
4. Listen effectively and take good lecture notes
5. Learn specialized and general vocabulary

6. Attend and participate in class
7. Utilize textbook organization, study aids, and publisher's study guides to improve reading comprehension and recall
8. Take reading notes
9. Highlight the text effectively
10. Prepare study sheets to achieve synthesis of ideas from many sources; for example, from notes, text, labs, etc. (Wood 1977)
11. Effectively prepare for and take essay tests
12. Effectively prepare for and take short answer tests
13. Use SQ3R or a similar study system which incorporates self-questioning on the material to be learned
14. For research assignments, use systematic research techniques and appropriate form for footnotes, bibliography, and so on.

Coping With Deeper Attitude Problems

Negative attitudes such as discouragement, defensiveness, and resistance interfere with the student's learning and inhibit communication with the counselor. "What Works" can be used to help problems that have an emotional basis. This is an important issue for academic counselors, who seldom have professional psychological credentials.

Through "What Works," the counselor focuses on the present problem and the resources within this student's experience and this college which can be tapped to solve the immediate problem. In so doing, the counselor helps the student to make contact with those persons who can assist the student further. Some students may need the help of a therapist. The vast majority of students, however, develop more positive attitudes as they work out effective solutions to their immediate academic crises.

Within the counselor's repertoire are the following coping skills which students may develop using the "What Works" dialogue.

1. See appropriate college personnel to clarify and specify the *exact* nature of the academic problem, demand, assignment, reason for failure, etc. These persons may include the instructor, the faculty advisor, the division chairman, the deans. Going to see a faculty member in his or her office may seem an enormous hurdle to the student in difficulty, yet this step and the ensuing communication are essential to defining the problem and developing a solution. This visit in the office (not a hasty contact before or after class) is often a stimulus to change. The counselor can help the student set up a conference and plan an approach to the faculty member.
2. Reconsider course and curriculum decisions with advisors. Student interests frequently change, yet new students in the college may not know whom to see to explore alternatives. The counselor encourages plans that include exploratory visits to other faculty, advisors, or peer counselors whose major field is in the student's tentative interest area.

3. Seek help from others to clarify personal goals. Changes of interest, loss of interest, and uncertainty are not abnormal or hopeless conditions. Rather they are typical problems which are amenable to solution through the appropriate kinds of activities. Academic counselors should be familiar with the current counseling center schedule of workshops, career counseling activities, and other such events.
4. Get professional help for serious emotional problems. A counselor may guide a student to such helpful professionals as a chaplain, personal counselor, psychiatrist, or the dean of students.

POSTSCRIPT

None of us—students or educators—choose the era in which we live. We cannot change the predominant culture, nor can many of us make sweeping changes in the institutions within which we study and educate. In our role as academic counselors, however, we can control the ground rules for our interactions with students. Inevitably, whether we intend to or not, we will encourage our students either to perpetuate dependency or to assume greater responsibility for their own learning. The "What Works" method enables academic counselors to directly influence this all important outcome and to foster self-reliant learner responses even while helping students overcome their learning problems.

REFERENCES

Chickering, A. W. 1969. *Education and identity.* San Francisco: Jossey-Bass.

Keimig, R. T. 1983. *Raising academic standards: a guide to learning improvement.* ASHE-ERIC/Higher Education Report No. 4. Washington, D. C.: Association for the Study of Higher Education.

Levine, A. 1980. *When dreams and heroes died: a portrait of today's college student.* San Francisco: Jossey-Bass.

Maxwell, M. 1979. *Improving student learning skills.* San Francisco: Jossey-Bass.

Millman, J., and Pauk, W. J. 1969. *How to take tests.* New York: McGraw-Hill.

Ozer, M. N. 1980. *Solving learning and behavior problems of children.* San Francisco: Jossey-Bass.

Roueche, J. E., Mink, O. G., and Armes, N. 1981. Coaching against helplessness in the classroom. *Community and Junior College Journal.* 51: 36-38.

Roueche, J. E., and Snow, G. J. 1977. *Overcoming learning problems.* San Francisco: Jossey-Bass.

Simmons, R. et al. 1979. *Teaching the disadvantaged in engineering.* ERIC ED 180:356.

Whimbey, A., and Lockhead, J. 1981. *Problem solving and comprehension: a short course in analytical reasoning*, 2nd ed. Philadelphia: The Frank-

lin Institute.
Wood, N. V. 1977. *College reading and study skills.* New York: Holt, Rinehart and Winston.

Thinking About "What Works"

Elizabeth F. Swanson, EdD

Education derives from the Latin word, *educere*, which means "to lead forth." This classical meaning contradicts the current state of education in which teachers typically assume the primary role in the teaching and learning process. While lip service is paid to the concept of students as "active" learners, all too often the typical class consists of a large proportion of teacher talk and very little student activity beyond assigned seatwork. Regardless of what is proclaimed among educators, the process of classroom education as it currently exists consists of learners as a passive audience (Goodlad 1983). Most teachers act as technicians, who give information and expect that students will absorb it. This traditional teaching process is not much more complicated than adding oil to an engine to insure that it will continue to run smoothly. Likewise, traditional instruction offers little to those students who do not already perform well. While many teachers have mastered specific skills in teaching, only a very few have mastered the art of leading students forth to accomplish their own learning.

This book calls for a return to education as a creative interaction between teacher and student, an interaction which results in the increased use of student resources and intellect. This book views education as a process of "leading forth," where teacher and students have separate but equally important responsibilities. The teacher acts as a guide and model, whose authority rests upon knowledge, experience, and the ability to analyze and solve those problems in life which lead to effective learning. The teacher also has skills in orchestrating the educational environment in such a way as to encourage students to learn, to grow, and to assume responsibility for their own problem solving and learning. The teacher both directs (structures) and shares in the learning process. Students in turn assume more responsibility for knowing the demands of a given task, for understanding how they learn, for monitoring their learning, and for meeting the mastery requirements as established by the teacher and by the curriculum.

Most teachers would agree that this description of education is an ideal that they strive toward. In the same breath, however, they would say that this ideal cannot be achieved given today's classroom realities. Many reasons are suggested for this perceived failure: "Students are too unruly. They don't care. Parents don't support us. I have too much material to cover. I would lose control of my class. We need to get back-to-basics anyway and make them learn."

These are reasonable concerns. Matters of discipline do pose a problem in schools today. Perhaps with more couples in which both parents work and with more one-parent families, there is less interaction between school and home. Also, there is the problem that more content is added to the curriculum each year, with such topics as environmental pollution, drug education, and nuclear energy competing with the more traditional units of study. An additional pressure on teachers is the movement to tighten graduation requirements and raise academic standards.

These trends in education have increased teacher workload and created an urgent need for approaches to teaching that place more responsibility for learning on students. In fact, it is likely that the sharing of educational responsibilities with students will allow educators to respond more effectively to the increasingly complex demands placed upon school systems. Students who assume responsibility for their academic progress are less likely to have behavior problems than students who simply react to the teacher and the educational environment. A joint effort between teacher and student to learn can lead to greater academic accomplishments than a traditional setting where teachers attempt to exert more authority than students (or society) are willing to grant. As students play a more active role in the educational process, teachers can experience more success and satisfaction in their jobs.

LEARNING CHARACTERISTICS OF STUDENTS WHO DO NOT ACHIEVE

Not all students spontaneously demonstrate the skills that are necessary to learn efficiently in school. These skills do not develop in children without assistance. Parents generally are models for the use of learning strategies, even from a very early age. Parents playing with a child help him to complete a difficult puzzle by talking about the various clues that each piece provides. This modeling can take the form of questions to help the child monitor what he is doing (e.g., What part of the picture do you see in this piece of puzzle?), help the child plan (e.g., What pieces are missing? What do you think this will be a picture of when you are finished?), and help the child by providing feedback after the child has executed a task (e.g., You finished the whole puzzle by yourself!). Corrective feedback is given in day-to-day activities as children learn to dress themselves, brush their own teeth, and assume more responsibility for their own daily care.

Children who are not provided with clear models for approaching new learning opportunities may well have difficulty relating to learning tasks in school. Because appropriate learning strategies have not become internalized in immature children, they may not be used spontaneously or successfully in the school setting.

Recent research in the use of different learning strategies offers us some information about the varied problem solving characteristics of many students who do not succeed in school.

- Some problem learners are unable to plan an approach to a given problem or learning task, to monitor their progress, and to check the results (Brown and Palincsar 1982; Campione and Brown 1977; Torgesen 1977, 1982).
- Many mildly retarded and learning disabled students fail to use such techniques as mentally categorizing objects in order to remember them, even at an age when this would be both appropriate and expected of them (Torgesen 1979).
- Some problem learners show developmental delays in their ability to recall information by verbally repeating or rehearsing words or phrases to themselves as a means of reinforcement (Tarver, Hallahan, Cohen, and Kauffman 1977; Tarver, Hallahan, Kauffman, and Ball 1976).
- Slow or retarded learners and problem readers have difficulty estimating the degree of difficulty of a task or even in noticing that they are experiencing difficulty (Brown 1982; Garner and Taylor 1982; Markham 1977).

One might think that these learning strategies that children acquire through development, experience, and the assistance of adults would be well instilled and efficiently used by adulthood. This is not so. Even at the high school and college levels, students who are inefficient learners may require extensive instruction in such strategies as outlining and note-taking before they will use these skills effectively (Brown and Smiley 1978). Applying efficient learning strategies often does not occur spontaneously even in adult learners.

Students who know certain learning strategies may not apply them when they are needed. There is not always a direct relationship between what one knows about learning and what one does about it. For example, knowing that writing down a word will aid recall does not mean a student will use this strategy. The student may not yet have made the connection between learning a particular strategy in one situation and applying it consistently in other instances where it will also be effective. Some students may not monitor their own responses (e.g., in reading); they ignore confused meanings which should signal a need for some problem-solving activity to correct the confusion. Furthermore, a student may not choose to use a particular learning strategy, believing that a less time-consuming method will work just as well. One study found that though a group of children indicated that categorizing words would help them to memorize the words, there were some who used the strategy and some who did not (Salatas and Flavell 1976). The consistent and efficient use of learning strategies varies with many circumstances, including the type of task, the degree to which the strategies were learned, the difficulty of the task, and the motivation of the learner.

Some children experiencing learning problems have more difficulty than others applying the strategies they already know to the appropriate learning activities. In fact, many performance deficiencies that once were thought to arise from structural deficiencies (e.g., mental retardation, minimal brain dysfunction), may be simply the inefficient use of strategies (Bos and Filip 1984; Torgesen 1980; Wiens 1983). While handicapped students were not lacking in their ability to master learning strategies, they needed instruction in their use. The following show examples of this point.

- When learning disabled children and normal children were asked to remember serially presented items, the learning disabled children demonstrated poorer performance and used fewer strategies for remembering, such as labeling the objects or verbally rehearsing the list. But performance improved after these students were instructed in the verbal rehearsal strategy (Tarver et. al. 1976).
- When groups of poor and average readers in fourth grade were asked to recall 24 pictures of common objects that could be grouped into four conceptual categories, the poor readers remembered fewer pictures and used fewer strategies for memorization. The better readers moved the pictures around more, grouping them into conceptual categories. They also verbalized the picture names more often and showed more on-task behavior (or less off-task behavior). Brief training in the categorization strategy eliminated differences in recall between the two reading groups (Torgesen 1977).

This is not to say that all students who have learning difficulties in school need only to be taught certain learning strategies; however, because many problem learners develop these learning strategies at a slower rate than their normally achieving peers, their ability is improved when assistance is given in applying these strategies and when there are consistent problem-solving models throughout their educational experience (Brown 1982; Ozer 1980).

When students are helped to learn specific strategies, improvement occurs on these particular tasks. Unfortunately, all too often these learned strategies do not generalize to new or related tasks where the same strategy would be appropriate (Meichenbaum 1979; Brown 1982). This is an unfortunate but significant drawback to the approach of teaching specific strategies for particular, isolated tasks.

NEED FOR A GENERAL PROBLEM-SOLVING APPROACH

To be proficient at self-directed learning and problem solving, students must have knowledge not only of specific learning strategies but of a systematic method for approaching a learning task. They must know about their own capabilities and learning characteristics. This includes skills of estimating the difficulty of a particular task, evaluating a task on the basis of what strategies can be applied to it, being able to monitor the use of strategies, breaking down the task into manageable units, and using feedback or evaluation to determine whether the approach was successful. These combined skills provide the framework for learning within which a variety of specific learning strategies operate. Students must have this more general problem-solving orientation in order to apply learned skills to all tasks effectively.

The need for a broader approach to solving problems is becoming more recognized in education today (Meichenbaum 1979; Taylor 1983). Brown and Palincsar (1982, p. 14) describe training in this area.

> Ideal cognitive skills training programs would include practice in the specific task-appropriate strategies (skills training); instruction in the orchestration, overseeing, and monitoring of those skills (self-regulation training); and information concerning the significance of those activities and their range of utility (awareness training). The level of intervention needed will depend critically on the preexisting knowledge and experience of the learner and the complexity of the procedures being taught.

Training must be in depth, occur throughout the student's learning environment, assist with the development of a plan for approaching and mastering learning tasks, provide an opportunity for the student to learn from evaluation of the strategies applied, and must promote use of the strategy in a variety of appropriate learning tasks. To use a computer analogy, effective problem solving means assisting the student in his own self-programming.

THE JOB OF EDUCATORS

The need for a systematic problem solving approach to learning is not limited to the student population. Research literature on effective teaching is replete with data about the importance of improved problem-solving skills among teachers (Becher, Hillmeier, Reisbeck, and Strohner 1979; Hunter 1979; Moore, Schaut, and Fritzges 1978; Shavelson 1982). Just as students must master the learning environment, so must teachers. They must use the same systematic approach to the difficult task of mastering the curriculum. This job requires that teachers be "students of students." McDonald (1977, p. 30) draws the following conclusions about the skills of teachers:

> Professional competence assumes that teaching involves continuous problem solving. Pupils differ considerably in their interests, motivation, aptitudes, and rate of learning. Given the variety of educational goals to be achieved, the variety of human beings to be taught, it is unlikely the same instructional procedures will work for all students; at best, a particular instructional procedure may work for a group, class, or type of student. Therefore, the teacher must engage in a complex and adaptive form of problem solving.

Teachers must be able to recognize a problem that a student is having, know when their intervention is needed, estimate the extent and dynamics of the problem, develop a plan of instruction, draw upon appropriate teaching strategies, monitor their use, evaluate the results of the instructional plan, and develop appropriate new plans. Teaching is an ongoing process, as all learning is.

There is evidence to suggest that training teachers to use specific instructional strategies in one setting, such as a college classroom or a teaching clinic, does not mean that the teachers will apply these techniques to their own classroom environment (McDonald 1977). The orchestration and integration of teaching strategies is not automatic. Assistance is needed to help teachers apply the strategies they learn to the actual classroom setting (Haberman 1980).

The problem of transfer of instructional strategies to appropriate situations parallels the problem of teaching specific learning strategies to poor learners who do not generalize them to new and related experiences. If generalization is to occur among teachers who have been taught a variety of strategies to work with problem learners, and if teachers are to be flexible in their instructional approaches with all students, they must have a general framework from which they can appropriately select and monitor the use of their applied teaching strategies. Teachers who limit their instructional strategies and do not use other approaches are likely to be lacking in a more general strategic approach to teaching. This general strategic approach (problem-solving orientation) is the key to effectiveness and flexibility in the classroom. Furthermore, to model systematic problem-solving approaches to learning is to teach self-directed learning to students.

Multidisciplinary teams are no different from teachers with respect to the use of problem-solving behavior. Their job is to assist teachers in the process of determining how certain students can best be taught to learn for themselves and manage more effectively their own achievement. This is a dynamic process which need not be limited to reporting specialized test scores and the development of plans that meet primarily administrative requirements.

To teach students how to become responsible and self-directed learners, educators must themselves assume the learner role. Educators are students of the learning process itself, drawing from their own resources that which they know will be useful to them in each new instructional challenge. And in practicing a more strategic systematic problem-solving approach to the instruction of students, educators begin to model the deeper meaning of the word *education*, "to lead forth." By use of example and problem-solving dialogue, teachers help students to become active, self-directed learners. Both educators and students then assume mutual responsibility for the teaching and learning process.

THE "WHAT WORKS" METHOD

The chapters of this book have described the "What Works" method as an approach to instruction, planning, and team problem solving. This system provides a general framework within which specific strategies for learning or instruction can be applied. It is a method for identifying a student's learning problem, for becoming aware of what has worked successfully in the past, for determining what approaches to a problem's solution can best be taken, and for developing a plan of action. The "What Works" method also generalizes learning by being global enough to be applied in a variety of instructional settings and tasks, and by focusing on the selection and application of strategies specifically successful to the learner.

The "What Works" method provides the teacher with a method to mediate learning in students. This ongoing problem-solving dialogue between teacher and student embodies a structure for learning which gradually becomes internalized by students.

In fact, the "What Works" method differs from other cognitive problem-solving strategies in a significant way: The "What Works" strategies increasingly derive from the student because the question "What Works?" is for the user to learn to answer for himself. To the degree that the student can generate or adopt new strategies that are successful, to this degree does he achieve independence in learning. A student who uses the "What Works" method has an ever-growing repertoire of learning strategies and an ever-increasing flexibility and efficiency in the whole learning process. This book demonstrates through reporting of actual field experiences that students can learn to monitor their own learning just as educators can learn to draw more effectively upon their own experience and inner resources. The result is greater self-sufficiency among both teachers and students and a more balanced responsibility in the educational process.

REFERENCES

Becker, B., Hillmeier, H., Reisbeck, G., and Strohner, H. 1979. Behaviour theory in the nursery school: problem solving and teacher training. *International Review of Education* 25:501-515.

Bos, C. S., and Filip, D. 1984. Comprehension monitoring in learning disabled and average students. *Journal of Learning Disabilities* 17:4, pp. 229-233.

Brown, A. L. 1982. Learning how to learn from reading. In *Reader Meets Author / Bridging the Gap: A Psycholinguistic and Sociolinguistic Perspective*, ed. J. A. Langer and M. T. Smith-Burke, pp. 26-54. Newark, Delaware: International Reading Association.

Brown, A. L., and Palincsar, A. S. 1982. Inducing strategic learning from texts by means of informed, self-control training. *Topics in Learning and Learning Disabilities* 2:1, pp. 1-17.

Brown, A. L., and Smiley, S. S. 1978. The development of strategies for studying texts. *Child Development* 49:1076-1088.

Campione, J. C., and Brown, A. L. 1977. Memory and metamemory development in educable retarded children. In *Perspectives on the development of memory and cognition*, ed. R. Kail and J. Hagen, pp. 367-403. Hillsdale, N.J.: Laurence Erlbaum Associates.

Garner, R., and Taylor, N. E. 1982. Monitoring of understanding: an investigation of attentional assistance needs at different grade and reading proficiency levels. *Reading Psychology* 3:1-6.

Goodlad, J. I. 1983. A study of schooling: some implications for school improvement. *Phi Delta Kappan* 64:8, pp. 552-558.

Haberman, M. 1980. Principles of inservice training for implementing mainstreaming in the public schools. In *Special education in transition: concepts to guide the education of experienced teachers*, ed. D. C. Corrigan and K. R. Howey, pp. 53-64. Reston, Virginia: The Council for Exceptional Children.

Hunter, M. 1979. Teaching is decision making. *Educational Leadership* 37:1, pp. 62-67.

Markman, E. M. 1977. Realizing that you don't understand: a preliminary investigation. *Child Development* 48:986-992.

McDonald, F. J. 1977. Research and development strategies for improving teacher education. *Journal of Teacher Education* 28:6, pp. 29-33.

Meichenbaum, D. 1979. Teaching children self-control. In *Advances in clinical child psychology* vol. 2, ed. B. B. Lahey and A. E. Kazden, pp. 1-33. New York: Plenum Press.

Moore, J. W., Schaut, J., and Fritzges, C. 1978. Evaluation of the effects of feedback associated with a problem-solving approach to instruction on teacher and student behavior. *Journal of Educational Psychology* 70:2, pp. 200-208.

Ozer, M. N. 1980. *Solving learning and behavior problems of children.* San Francisco: Jossey-Bass.

Salatas, H., and Flavell, J. H. 1976. Behavioral and metamnemonic indicators of strategic behaviors under remember instructions in first grade. *Child Development* 47:81-89.

Shavelson, R. J. 1982. *Review of research on teachers' pedagogical judgments, plans and decisions.* Washington, D. C.: The National Institute of Education.

Tarver, S. G., Hallahan, D. P., Cohen, S. B., and Kauffman, J. M. 1977. The development of visual selective attention and verbal rehearsal in learning disabled boys. *Journal of Learning Disabilities* 10:8, pp. 491-500.

Tarver, S. G., Hallahan, D. P., Kauffman, J. M., and Ball, D. W. 1976. Verbal rehearsal and selective attention in children with learning disabilities: a developmental lag. *Journal of Experimental Child Psychology* 22: 375-385.

Taylor, N. E. 1983. Metacognitive ability: a curriculum priority. *Reading Psychology* 4:269-287.

Torgesen, J. K. 1977. Memorization processes in reading-disabled children. *Journal of Educational Psychology* 69:5, pp. 571-578.

Torgesen, J. K. 1980. Conceptual and educational implications of the use of efficient task strategies by learning disabled children. *Journal of Learning Disabilities* 13:7, pp. 364-371.

Torgesen, J. K. 1982. The learning disabled child as an inactive learner: educational implications. *Topics in Learning and Learning Disabilities* 2:1, pp. 45-52.

Torgesen, J. K., Murphy, H. A., and Ivey, C. 1979. The influence of an orienting task on the memory performance of children with reading problems. *Journal of Learning Disabilities* 12:6, pp. 396-407.

Wiens, J. W. 1983. Metacognition and the adolescent passive learner. *Journal of Learning Disabilities* 16:3, pp. 144-149.

The Authors

Elizabeth Barger, EdD, directs a reading clinic and is a reading specialist in Washington County Public Schools, Maryland. She works with regular teachers to improve the instruction of students experiencing learning problems in the regular setting. Address: 38 Woodside Drive, Hagerstown, Maryland 21740.

Ruth Harris is the director of the Northwest Reading Clinic in Eau Claire, Wisconsin. She has master's degrees in reading disabilities, learning disabilities, and emotional disturbance. She taught in the public schools as a regular elementary teacher, and currently works with students of all ages who are experiencing learning problems. Ms. Harris served as the vice president of the Eau Claire, Wisconsin, School Board for several terms, was a reading consultant to the University of Wisconsin, Eau Claire, and has given workshops and presentations about learning and reading disabilities at the local, state, and national levels. Address: 1027 East Grant Avenue, Eau Claire, Wisconsin 54701.

Ruth Talbott Kemig, EdD, refined the use of the "What Works" method for study skills teaching and also developed the peer counselor training program during a recent five year stint as dean of freshmen in a metropolitan four-year college. She is presently a reading specialist with Calvert County, Maryland, public schools and a consultant to other school systems and colleges. Dr. Kemig is the author of *Raising Academic Standards: A Guide to Learning Improvement*, published in 1983 by the Association for the Study of Higher Education in their research report series. She can be reached at the following address: Kemig Associates Incorporated, P.O. Box 449, Lusby, Maryland 20657.

Harriet Liebow is Assistant in Special Education, Charles County Public Schools, Maryland. She coordinates the Maryland State Department of Education Learning Disabilities Project in team decision-making, develops curriculum materials, and does inservice training of teachers.

Mark N. Ozer, MD, is at present an associate professor of neurology at the Medical College of Virginia in Richmond. When the work was done upon which this book was based, Dr. Ozer was an associate professor of child health and development at the George Washington School of Medicine in Washington, D.C. He has written extensively on his work with children who have learning and behavioral problems, including over 50 articles in the professional literature, and has consulted in a variety of educational settings throughout the country on techniques described in this book. Recent books include: *A Cybernetic Approach to Assessment: Toward a More Humane Use of Human Beings* (Westview Press 1979); *Solving Learning and Behavior Problems of Children* (Jossey-Bass 1980); and *The Ozer Method: A Problem Solving Technique for Parents and Children* (William Morrow Co. 1982).

Nancy Smith, PhD, is the supervisor of staff development in Charles County Public Schools, Maryland. She has been a classroom teacher, principal, and instructor at Johns Hopkins University and Goucher College. She currently supervises teachers and conducts inservice training.

Elizabeth F. Swanson, EdD, started her career as a special education resource teacher in a succession of elementary, middle, and secondary schools. She has worked with regular teachers through team teaching, inservice training, and as an instructor at the University of Maryland and at Catholic University of America. She is currently in private practice and is doing workshops, evaluations of students' learning styles, and computer-assisted tutoring. Her research projects include software evaluation and development of techniques for better teaching and learning. Address: 322 N.W. 74th Street, Seattle, Washington 98117.